Mastering the Basic Math Facts in Addition and Subtraction

Mastering the Basic Math Facts in Addition and Subtraction

Strategies, Activities & Interventions to Move Students Beyond Memorization

Susan O'Connell and John SanGiovanni

HEINEMANN
Portsmouth, NH

Heinemann

361 Hanover Street

Portsmouth, NH 03801–3912

www.heinemann.com

Offices and agents throughout the world

Library of Congress Cataloging-in-Publication Data

O'Connell, Susan.

Mastering the basic math facts in addition and subtraction : strategies, activities & interventions to move students beyond memorization / Susan O'Connell and John SanGiovanni.

    p. cm.

  Includes bibliographical references.

  ISBN-13: 978-0-325-02963-4

  ISBN-10: 0-325-02963-6

  1. Addition—Study and teaching (Primary). 2. Subtraction—Study and teaching (Primary). I. SanGiovanni, John. II. Title.

  QA115 .O33 2011

  372.7'2—dc22

                                    2010046911

Editor: Victoria Merecki

Production: Victoria Merecki

Cover and interior designs: Palmer Creative Group

Composition: Publishers' Design and Production Services, Inc.

Manufacturing: Steve Bernier

Printed in the United States of America on acid-free paper

15   14   13   12   11   VP   1   2   3   4   5

Contents

Foreword   **xiii**

Acknowledgments   **xv**

Introduction   **1**

    What are basic facts?   1

    What constitutes *mastery* of basic facts?   2

    Why do we need to know basic facts?   2

    Why is it important to understand math facts?   3

    How can we help students master basic math facts?   5

    How can this book help you?   7

    How is this book organized?   8

    What is the teaching sequence of math facts within this book?   9

    Why are activities and resources on a CD?   12

    Resource for Professional Learning Communities   13

    Our Goal   13

CHAPTER 1   **Understanding Addition and Subtraction**   **15**

    Exploring Big Ideas to Develop Math Fact Strategies   16

    Building Understanding Prior to Focusing on Fluency   18

    Using Models to Represent Addition and Subtraction   18

    Exploring the Concepts of Addition and Subtraction Through Problems   23

    Exploring Operations Through Children's Literature   25

    Partner Explorations   26

    The Classroom Environment   27

    Beginning with Understanding   29

CHAPTER 2 **Plus One and Plus Two**   **31**

Focusing on the Big Ideas   32

Understanding +1, +2 Facts   34

    Literature Link: *Mouse Count*   34

    Exploring the Facts: Number Strips to Visualize 1 More and 2 More   38

    Supporting All Learners   39

Building Automaticity   41

    Targeted Practice   42

    Monitoring Progress   45

Connecting to Subtraction   46

CHAPTER 3 **Adding Zero**   **51**

Focusing on the Big Ideas   52

Understanding +0 Facts   53

    Literature Link: *Gray Rabbit's 1, 2, 3*   53

    Exploring the Facts: Acting Out +0 Facts   54

    Supporting All Learners   56

Building Automaticity   58

    Targeted Practice   58

    Monitoring Progress   60

Connecting to Subtraction   60

CHAPTER 4 **Adding Ten**   **63**

Focusing on the Big Ideas   64

Understanding +10 Facts   65

Literature Link: *If You Give a Mouse a Cookie*　　　65

Exploring the Facts: Using Double Ten-Frames　　　66

Supporting All Learners　　　68

Building Automaticity　　　70

Targeted Practice　　　70

Monitoring Progress　　　72

Connecting to Subtraction　　　72

CHAPTER 5　Doubles　　　77

Focusing on the Big Ideas　　　78

Understanding Doubles　　　78

Literature Link: *Double the Ducks*　　　78

Exploring the Facts: Creating Equal Sets　　　81

Supporting All Learners　　　82

Building Automaticity　　　85

Targeted Practice　　　85

Monitoring Progress　　　88

Connecting to Subtraction　　　88

CHAPTER 6　Making Ten　　　93

Focusing on the Big Ideas　　　94

Understanding Making Ten　　　95

Literature Link: *Ten Apples up on Top!*　　　95

Exploring the Facts: The Cupcake Problem　　　97

Supporting All Learners　　　98

Building Automaticity   101

    Targeted Practice   101

    Monitoring Progress   106

Connecting to Subtraction   107

CHAPTER 7   **Using Tens**   **111**

Focusing on the Big Ideas   113

Understanding Using Tens   114

    Literature Link: *Diary of a Worm*   114

    Exploring the Facts: Counters In and Out   117

    Supporting All Learners   118

Building Automaticity   121

    Targeted Practice   121

    Monitoring Progress   123

Connecting to Subtraction   124

CHAPTER 8   **Using Doubles**   **127**

Focusing on the Big Ideas   128

Understanding Using Doubles   129

    Literature Link: *Fish Eyes*   129

    Exploring the Facts: Doubles and One More   131

    Supporting All Learners   132

Building Automaticity   134

    Targeted Practice   134

    Monitoring Progress   136

Connecting to Subtraction   137

One Lonely Fact   140

Retaining Math Facts   140

Automatic Recall of Facts   142

Conclusion   **143**

References   **145**

Professional References   145

Children's Literature   145

Professional Learning Communities Study Guide   **147**

Guiding Questions   149

A Guide to the CD-ROM   **155**

Organization of the CD Files   155

Teaching Resources   155

Teaching Tools   155

Fact Cards   155

Assessment Tools   156

Modifications to CD Activities   156

Foreword

Being able to add and subtract within 20 and multiply and divide within 100 is essential during the early years of schooling, and the basic facts of addition/subtraction and multiplication/division are a critical baseline, not only then but also during later work with fractions, decimals, ratio, proportion, and more. Foundational? You better believe it. Essential? Absolutely.

That said, the basic facts are also problematic. The goal is for most students to know, fluently, and with automaticity, the addition/subtraction facts, typically by the end of second grade and the multiplication/division facts, typically by the end of third grade. But far too many teachers are unable to help their students reach these goals. "Not this year," they may mutter, or, "Not all my students," or worse, "Not ever." Why is fluency with the basic facts such a challenge for so many students? In our digit-conscious culture students can spout off multiple phone and pin numbers, but not the product of 6×7! I meet and work with middle school students who are still wondering about 8×7 or $48 \div 6$ and other basic facts. Why do far too many students fail to realize that the commutative property means that $9 + 7$ and $7 + 9$ get you to the same place, 16? This drives us all crazy! Have we neglected the basics? Is this about just having students memorize the facts? No, and no!

Over twenty years ago the *Curriculum and Evaluation Standards for School Mathematics* noted that "children should master the basic facts of arithmetic that are essential components of fluency with paper-pencil and mental computation and with estimation" (47).[1] The National Research Council's *Adding It Up* dedicates almost ten pages to synthesizing the research dealing with basic fact acquisition.[2] More recently, the *Final Report of the National Mathematics Advisory Panel* points out that computational proficiency with whole number operations depends on the practice (I prefer the term *rehearsal*) necessary to develop automatic recall of addition/subtraction and multiplication/division facts.[3] Nurturing computational facility in elementary school requires that students be fluent with the basic facts of arithmetic. How do we get this done?

---

[1] National Council of Teachers of Mathematics. 1989. *Curriculum and Evaluation Standards for School Mathematics.* Reston, VA: National Council of Teachers of Mathematics.

[2] National Research Council. 2001. *Adding It Up: Helping Children Learn Mathematics.* Washington, DC: National Academy Press.

[3] National Mathematics Advisory Panel. 2008. *Foundations for Success: The Final Report of the National Mathematics Advisory Panel.* Washington, DC: U.S. Department of Education.

Over the years teachers have tried and continue to use a myriad of practice activities—oral and written exercises, games, and classroom and homework assignments, many of them now via the Internet. At last we have a more effective option—Susan O'Connell and John SanGiovanni's *Mastering the Basic Facts in Addition and Subtraction: Strategies, Activities & Interventions to Move Students Beyond Memorization* and *Mastering the Basic Facts in Multiplication and Division: Strategies, Activities & Interventions to Move Students Beyond Memorization*. What a find!

Based on Thornton's pioneering work[4] emphasizing how thinking strategies facilitate fact acquisition, both books present activities that develop facility with the basic facts by building a conceptual understanding of the operations; following a teaching sequence designed to develop a sense of number using fact strategies and the commutative property; and using representational models and context-based problem solving. (The activities that link facts to their conceptual representations are also powerful diagnostic tools.) But there's more—related children's literature, partner activities, a professional-learning-community study guide. All these components add up to resources that engage students, from beginning activities that promote an understanding of arithmetic concepts, through fluency with the basic facts.

One final consideration: these books will be very helpful to teachers whose students' mathematical knowledge require some level of intervention. The powerful instructional opportunities these books provide not only make sense but also meet one of the key recommendations of the What Works Clearinghouse's Practice Guide *Assisting Students Struggling with Mathematics*.[5]

These books won't end up on a shelf at the back of your room. (And if you are a third/fourth-grade teacher you will probably need both of them.) You'll use them every day. You'll carry them home with you and talk about them in the faculty lounge. Just as the basic facts are "must haves" on the path to computational fluency, these books are "must haves" to help you navigate the route.

Francis (Skip) Fennell

L. Stanley Bowlsbey Professor of Education & Graduate and Professional Studies

McDaniel College, Westminster, MD

Past President, National Council of Teachers of Mathematics

Project Director, Elementary Mathematics Specialists and Teacher Leaders Project

http://mathspecialists.org

---

4 Thornton, C.A. 1978. "Emphasizing Thinking Strategies in Basic Fact Instruction." *Journal for Research in Mathematics Education*. 16: 337–355.

5 Gersten et al. 2009. *Assisting Students Struggling with Mathematics: Response to Intervention (RtI) for Elementary and Middle Schools*. Washington, DC: Institute of Education Sciences.

Acknowledgments

Many thanks to the students whose conversations about math facts inspired and excited us as we worked on this manuscript. Thanks to the following students who contributed work samples or allowed their photographs to appear within this book: Samantha Anderson, Jack Bacon, Julia Basket, Riley Benson, Justus Black, Krysta Carte, Eric Chen, Mason Chizhik, Esme Chu, Anessa Coleman, Ben Dyer, Nolan Dyer, Eric Ellis, Satya Emerick, Jonah Eng, Maximillian Fagerstrom, Anna Farley, Maya Frye, Emily Gomez, Maggie Inskeep, Ashley Jeon, Megan Keeley, Christopher Kennedy, Alexandra Liberto, DJ Lindahl, Emerson Mako, Caitlyn McDonald, Brooke Miller, Joshua Morton, Adam Mostafa, Brooke Naidu, Dylan Nguyen, Josh Oberly, Rona Okojie, Zion Olibris, Allison Peay, Jamie Roberts, Hannah Williams, Nushrat–I Rabban, Jack Ryder, Annie Schinkai, Sydney Schinkai, Oscar Schoenfelder, Deryn Schoenfelder, Lauren Stipe, Delaney Thompson, Laya Vanga, and Jilienne Widener. It was a pleasure watching them investigate math facts.

We appreciate the collaboration of colleagues in gathering materials for this book, in particular the following teachers, math coaches, and supervisors who welcomed us into their classrooms, provided insights from their own teaching, or allowed us to listen to the ideas of their students: Elizabeth Bare, Linda Chrest, Connie Conroy, Heather Dyer, Michelle Glenn, Carol Hahn, Renee Holdefelder, Ami Holden, Nena Hupp, Rhonda Inskeep, Arthurlea Kimbrough, Amanda Lewis, Kristen Mangus, Jamie Pickett, Kay Sammons, and Lee Ann Tanis. Thanks, too, to Josie Robles who had the inspiration to use ten-bead counters with her second grade students.

We are grateful to Victoria Merecki, our Heinemann editor, for her guidance on this project from start to finish. We value her insights for the writing and production of the book. In addition, we thank Emily Birch for her vision for this book. Her discussions in the early stages of the book were invaluable.

Special thanks to our families for their patience and understanding during the writing of this book. To Sue's husband Pat, and her children Brendan and Katie, and to John's wife Kristen, and Oscar and Deryn, our warmest thanks for your continued support.

Introduction

As math teachers, we want all of our students to develop a quick recall of single-digit addition and subtraction facts. We label them *basic* math facts because they provide a foundation for math success. We expect that all students will master these basic skills, but that is not a simple goal to achieve. We watch some students effortlessly remember the facts and others struggle with the very same task. And we labor to find just the right strategies and activities to help all students succeed.

As teachers, we are constantly reminded that our students learn in a variety of ways. Although some students have very strong memory skills, others struggle to remember simple facts. Although some students make sense of math concepts on their own, others struggle to connect meaning to simple expressions like 4 + 3. Although some students intuitively use their knowledge of one math fact to find the solution to a related fact, others simply get frustrated and discouraged when they cannot remember a specific sum. Our students are so different, and yet our goal for each of them is the same: to master basic math facts so they have a strong foundation for more complex math skills and procedures. The goal of this book is to explore numerous strategies and activities that support all students in understanding basic addition and subtraction math facts and committing those facts to memory. Whether you are introducing students to basic math facts, reviewing previously taught facts, or providing interventions for students who continue to struggle, this book supplies you with instructional considerations, teaching tips, practical strategies, and numerous classroom-tested activities.

What are basic facts?

In this book, facts with addends of 0–10 are considered basic facts. In some programs, facts with single-digit addends (0–9) are considered basic facts, but because of our emphasis on students' use of strategies when learning basic facts, we have included 10 as an addend. When adding 9 + 6, a student might reason that 10 + 6 = 16, so 9 + 6 is 1 less, or 15. That reasoning is not possible without an understanding of 10 as an addend. To ensure that students have the basic number understandings to reason in this way, addends of 0–10 are addressed. The strategies and activities within this book will focus on mastery of these basic math facts.

What constitutes *mastery* of basic math facts?

In the past, much of mathematics was taught in a drill and practice style. Students were simply asked to memorize their math facts, often without much attention to conceptual understanding. Through worksheets filled with single-digit computations or lengthy flash card sessions, students were asked to memorize addition and subtraction facts. Our goal in today's math classrooms has shifted from memorizing facts and procedures to increased understanding of math skills and concepts. We want our students to be able to do mathematics, but we also want them to understand the math they are doing. We recognize that as math tasks increase in complexity, an understanding of facts, formulas, and algorithms will help them experience continued success. We have not changed our view of the importance of basic math facts. We know that they are a foundational skill without which our students will view even simple math tasks as daunting. We have simply expanded our expectations to include understanding as an important component of our teaching of basic math facts. So, what do we expect of our students? Our goal is both automaticity and understanding. Automaticity is students' ability to effortlessly recall a fact. If students are automatic, they have successfully committed the facts to memory. In addition, we want our students to understand, not simply remember, these important math facts.

Why do we need to know basic math facts?

Ask math teachers what they would like their students to know and be able to do and the recall of basic math facts will undoubtedly rank high on most of their wish lists. Teachers recognize that once their students know $2 + 5$, those students are better able to explore $20 + 50$ or $22 + 55$. Teachers recognize that students will have an easier time finding the solution to $\$1.20 + \$1.50$ or $.21 + .53$. These teachers know that their students will be more successful when they are challenged with $\frac{2}{8} + \frac{5}{8}$. As math tasks become more complex, we want our students to have a solid foundation for success.

We have gained insights from brain research about demands on the working brain. As students begin to learn math facts, their brains are focused on these basic computations, but as students become automatic with basic facts, their brains are able to focus on other aspects of the task like the challenges of place value, decimals, or fractions. Being automatic with basic facts frees the brain to focus on other math processes.

Committing basic math facts to memory speeds up math tasks. As math tasks increase in complexity, they often require multiple steps to find the solution. Addition with three-digit addends and subtraction with decimals are examples of more complex computational tasks. These tasks are time-consuming, and often stressful, for students who must stop to figure out each basic fact along the way. And stopping to determine each fact disrupts the flow of the math procedure. The National Mathematics Advisory Panel (2008) urges that students develop automatic recall of addition and related subtraction facts to be prepared for the study of algebra, in which solving multistep equations is a fundamental task. The panel suggests that by the end of grade 3, students should be proficient with the addition and subtraction of whole numbers (National Mathematics Advisory Panel 2008).

Students who have committed basic math facts to memory are able to perform critical mental math tasks. They estimate answers prior to solving problems so they are able to compare their estimates to the actual answers and determine the reasonableness of their solutions. When playing a playground kickball game, students with mental math skills can determine the new game score after three more runs are scored, or can compare the team scores to figure out how many runs they will need to score in the final inning to win the game. As students spy a dozen cookies, they are able to quickly determine how many will be left after six are eaten, and students with a knowledge of math facts can efficiently find their total score in a family board game. Mastery of basic facts provides the foundation for everyday mental math tasks.

Automaticity is the quick and effortless recall of math facts. No need to count every object, no need to think about related facts, no need to extend patterns. The answer is automatically known. Automaticity with basic facts is a goal for our students, but alone it is not enough. Students must also understand the facts they are being asked to commit to memory.

Why is it important to understand math facts?

The ability to recall items is enhanced when understanding is connected to the task. Memorizing a chain of nonsensical words (e.g., *sat chair red girl a in little the*) is more difficult than memorizing a sentence in which the words have meaning (e.g., *A little girl sat in the red chair*). Asking students to memorize dozens of number facts can be discouraging and confusing when students view them simply as pairs of numbers. The understanding that 7 + 4 represents the combined total of those two quantities, and that the sum is clearly close to 10, aids our ability to recall the sum.

Students who simply memorize math facts miss a prime opportunity to expand their understanding of equations. Problem solving is the central focus in today's math classrooms. To be a successful problem solver, students must be able to accurately compute answers, but more than that, they must be able to figure out how to build equations that correspond to problem situations.

> Kellen's mother asked him to pick up the toy cars he left in the middle of the floor. He put 7 of them on top of his dresser. He put 6 more in his toy box. How many cars did he have?

This problem certainly requires the student to know that 7 + 6 = 13, but even before the student can use his knowledge of math facts to find the answer, he must understand how to build an equation that works with this problem.

> Some cars were placed on the dresser and others were placed in the toy box. I need to know how many he had altogether so I need to add. 7 + 6 will be how I find the answer.

As we discuss the connection between the meaning of the equation and the basic math fact, we are supporting both students' computation skills as well as building a strong foundation for problem solving.

Both the *Common Core State Standards* (National Governors Association Center for Best Practices and Council of Chief State School Officers 2010) and the National Council of Teachers of Mathematics' *Principles and Standards* (2000) emphasize the importance of our students understanding the concepts of addition and subtraction. The *Common Core State Standards* recommend that kindergarten students be given opportunities to explore addition as combining or adding to and subtraction as separating or taking away. Understanding is developed first, with practice for fluency coming later.

How can we help students master basic math facts?

We expect that our students will recall math facts without the need for manipulatives or counting strategies and that the recall will take place within several seconds. Certainly memorization of math facts is our goal, but memorization that comes from ongoing practice and engagement with math facts tasks, not memorization that comes from traditional drill and practice. And we recognize that our students benefit from varied opportunities to explore basic math facts before engaging in practice tasks designed to promote automatic recall. Through hands-on activities and thoughtful discussions, students develop deeper understandings about math facts and cultivate useful strategies related to these basic facts. An instructional approach in which students investigate the conceptual understanding of basic facts, explore strategies to support their understanding of numbers, and then engage in strategic practice in order to automatically recall the facts provides students with a strong and balanced foundation for mastery.

Conceptual Understanding

Understanding operations is fundamental to understanding math facts. Situations are symbolically represented by expressions. $2 + 5$ is more than numbers and symbols. The addition sign helps us understand the relationship between the numbers. $2 + 5$ represents the combined total of two quantities. The understanding of this relationship is critical to making sense of the expression. Through problem posing, hands-on explorations, real-world examples, classroom discussions, and exploring situations from children's literature, students develop deeper understandings of operations. An addition scenario that shows combined groups, or a subtraction story that shows comparisons, helps students strengthen their understanding of operations, and students who understand operations will find that math facts make sense.

Strategic Thinking

There are many ways that students might arrive at an answer to a math fact. When adding $8 + 3$, Jason might simply count every object being added, and Katie might simply remember that $8 + 3 = 11$. Math fact strategies lie somewhere between counting each object and simply memorizing the answer. They are predictable and efficient ways to find answers. Colin might *count on* beginning at 8 to say "8, *9, 10, 11*," while Liam knows that $8 + 2 = 10$ so $8 + 3$

must be 1 more than 10, or 11. Strategies help students find an answer even if they forget what was memorized. Teaching math fact strategies focuses attention on number sense, operations, patterns, properties, and other critical number concepts. These big ideas related to numbers provide a strong foundation for the strategic reasoning that supports mastering basic math facts. For addition and subtraction, understanding the concept of tens, knowing that the order of addends will not affect the sum, and recognizing that various numbers can create the same sum (e.g., 5 + 4 = 9 and 6 + 3 = 9) and that there is a unique relationship between those two equations (e.g., in the second expression, the first addend is one more and the second addend is one less) allows students to use their knowledge to build strategies to find sums and differences. Providing opportunities for students to explore math facts through active engagement and meaningful discussions builds their understanding of critical ideas about numbers (Fosnot and Dolk 2001; Gravemeijer and van Galen 2003; Van de Walle 2004) and is an important component of math fact mastery.

Practice for Fluency

Once an understanding of operations has been developed and students have explored strategic reasoning to find solutions to basic math facts, it is time to engage students in meaningful practice so they can commit the facts to memory. Rather than long practice sessions (Remember the lengthy flash card drills of days past?), consider activities that are short in duration but easy to implement, so you can frequently engage students in valuable practice. Scattered practice—five to ten minutes a day, spread throughout the school year—yields powerful results (Marzano, Pickering, and Pollock 2001). And varying the practice activities ensures that students stay motivated and engaged in learning their math facts. Automaticity is achieved through brief, frequent, interactive activities that provide students with repeated exposure to math facts.

Because of the anxiety associated with memorization tasks for many students, the practice tasks in this book do not focus on speed or elimination. Although speed drills or elimination games may be enjoyed by some students, these types of activities often intensify the frustration and anxiety of others. Students who struggle with rote memory tasks, those students who are the reason we include math fact activities in our daily schedule, are just the ones who become discouraged by the speed drills, experience humiliation when they are the first to be eliminated, and sit on the sidelines where they do not get the practice that they need.

There are multiple practice activities within this book that engage students in math fact practice without increasing their anxiety or allowing them to get discouraged. The practice tasks are interactive and hands-on, and provide students with repeated exposure to each set of math facts in a gradual progression in which each new set of facts builds on previous ones. Select the activities that work best for your students. Although some students might find competitive activities fun and motivating, others thrive on collegial tasks. Throughout this book, you will find activity choices to allow you to personalize math facts practice for your students.

How can this book help you?

This book is a practical guide for helping students master addition and subtraction facts. It includes insights into the teaching of basic math facts including a multitude of instructional strategies, teacher tips, and classroom activities designed to help students master their facts. The emphasis is on strengthening students' understanding of numbers, patterns, and properties as an essential component of math fact teaching. This book provides valuable resources, insights, and options to help you introduce your students to basic facts, provide reviews to support mastery, or develop interventions for students who have not yet mastered basic facts.

In this book, you will find activities and resources for introducing students to basic math facts. You will find tips for generating student talk about math facts including examples of questions and prompts that direct students' thinking toward big ideas and lead them to insights that will simplify the task of mastering the facts. You will find activities to support varied levels of learners so that you can choose the right activity to extend learning for high-level students or modify skills to support struggling students. You will find strategies that are hands-on, engaging, and interactive to motivate reluctant students. You will find activities perfect for small-group interventions and others that work well for whole-class instruction or individual support. And you will find a CD filled with resources to ease your planning and preparation.

This book is a compilation of strategies and activities that are organized to provide a solid math facts program; however, the individual activities and strategies can be easily integrated into your existing math program to provide you with additional resources and varied instructional approaches. You may read the book from start to finish or you may focus on specific sections that address your needs. Consider your students and select the strategies and activities to match their needs, interests, learning styles, and abilities.

How is this book organized?

Throughout the following chapters, a multitude of teaching strategies and activities are shared to build students' understanding and automaticity with math facts. Each chapter is organized to develop essential understanding and provide a menu of possible activities for instruction, practice, and assessment. Following are highlights of the key elements in Chapters 2 through 8.

Making Connections and Focusing on the Big Ideas

Each chapter begins by connecting the new fact set to students' previous experiences and provides a brief review of big ideas that play a key role in students' understanding of the facts and students' development of strategies related to the facts.

Developing Understanding

Each chapter provides two introductory lessons that focus on developing conceptual understanding of the highlighted math facts. One lesson is a Literature Link, introducing the facts through a story context. The other lesson, Exploring the Facts, provides a language-based and/or hands-on exploration of the new set of facts. The activities in this book employ varied instructional techniques, including the use of manipulatives, visuals, tables, literature, hundred charts, and discussions, ensuring that students experience addition and subtraction facts in diverse ways and that each student will be likely to experience these facts in a way that makes sense to him.

In Supporting All Learners, you will find more ideas for those students who may need additional or different types of experiences to develop understanding of the targeted facts. These activities might be done with the whole class but may also be perfect for small teacher-led groups of students. For some sets of facts, you may choose to use several of these activities; at other times, your students may not need the additional exposure. These activities simply provide you with more and varied possibilities for developing understanding.

Building Automaticity

This section focuses on building students' fluency and is broken into two parts: Targeted Practice and Monitoring Progress. In Targeted Practice, a variety of activities are shared that provide practice for that specific set of math facts. Students will have fun rolling number cubes, spinning spinners, and pulling number cards from a deck as they engage in ongoing practice through interactive activities. It is through repeated and targeted practice that students gain fluency with math facts. Templates for these activities can be found on the accompanying CD.

Along with repeated practice to gain fluency with math facts, students need constant monitoring to ensure that they are progressing in their mastery of facts. Monitoring Progress provides ideas for monitoring students' progress toward automaticity including ideas for conducting frequent fact checks, techniques for tracking students' progress, and suggestions for varied ways to monitor progress including student conferences, progress graphs, and individual goal setting.

Connecting to Subtraction

Addition facts are the primary emphasis throughout this book because of our focus on building math fact fluency. When posed with a subtraction math fact, the most efficient way to solve it is by knowing the related addition fact. When the recall of addition facts is automatic and students understand the connection between addition and subtraction facts, their fluency with subtraction facts naturally increases.

Lessons to develop students' understanding of related subtraction facts are included in each chapter. In addition, you will find suggestions throughout the book of activities to build subtraction fact fluency. To attain fluency with subtraction facts, students need ongoing opportunities to practice the facts and explore their connection to addition facts.

What is the teaching sequence of math facts within this book?

The chapters of this book are organized based on strategies that support students' understanding of addition and subtraction facts. These strategies allow students to make sense of math facts and, therefore, support their mastery of these facts. The strategies are based on big ideas about numbers and operations. The understanding of these big ideas helps students create effective math strategies related to the facts and to ultimately commit those facts to memory. This book is not simply a collection of activities; it is intended to highlight big ideas that provide a perfect focus for math facts instruction, to broaden your repertoire of instructional strategies, to provide you with dozens of easy-to-implement activity ideas, and to stimulate your reflection related to the teaching of math facts. In reviewing the organization of this book, you may notice that the math facts appear in a sequence that focuses on the complexity of the number concepts and carefully links each new set of facts to previously explored facts, building upon students' prior knowledge.

Rather than asking our students to memorize 121 combinations of addition facts and then 121 combinations of subtraction facts, this book focuses on helping students understand groups of facts and then building on that understanding with additional sets of facts. Over time, our students are given a strong foundation of number sense and number understanding.

Students begin by exploring facts that are one more and two more. These +1/+2 facts are linked to their counting experiences, as they are able to *count on* to find the sums. Exploring facts that are one less and two less allows students to investigate the addition/subtraction connection.

Once students have explored and begun to practice these facts, addition with zero is presented. Although the +0 facts are actually easier for automaticity than +1/+2 facts, the concept of joining is a bit harder to understand (What does it mean to add zero? Why do we add if we have nothing to add?). These facts are better addressed after students have had multiple experiences with +1/+2 facts and have developed the concept of addition.

Ten as an addend is explored next to allow students to develop automatic recall of +10 facts (e.g., $10 + 2 = 12$ or $4 + 10 = 14$). This skill will be critical later as students use +10 facts as a way of simplifying facts that are near 10 (e.g., $9 + 4$ is simplified to $10 + 3$).

Exploring doubles is addressed next. Through hands-on experiences, students explore the concept of doubling, find the sums of doubles, and begin to practice these facts for fluency. The automatic recall of doubles facts provides a foundation for more complex facts.

Next, students explore facts with a sum of 10. With 10 being central to our number system, students need many opportunities to explore ways to combine numbers to form 10. Once these facts are mastered, students have developed a strong foundation on which to build mastery of other facts. If students know that $8 + 2 = 10$, they can use that understanding to find the sum of $8 + 4$ or $8 + 5$.

Once our students have explored +1, +2, +0, +10, doubles, and making-ten facts, they have been exposed to the *foundation facts*. The remaining unknown facts can be found by building on this foundation. At this point, students have mastered 83 of the 121 addition facts. And they are armed with an understanding of tens and doubles, which will help them with their still unknown facts.

Using tens is a strategy that assists our students with sums that are near-ten facts. They have not yet explored $8 + 3$ but their knowledge that $8 + 2 = 10$ aids them. "It's 11 because 3 is just 1 more than 2 and $8 + 2 = 10$, so $8 + 3 = 11$!"

Next, our students explore more unknown facts using their doubles knowledge. Their previous experiences with doubles facts support students with more difficult facts like $6 + 7$. "I know $6 + 6 = 12$, so $6 + 7$ is just 1 more. It's 13!"

Through their known facts and their previously explored strategies, students now build mastery with the remaining facts. Although most of the basic facts have been connected to a specific strategy, it is important that students recognize the flexibility of these strategies, knowing that several strategies may work for a given fact. This flexibility allows students to find the answers for the two math facts that have not been specifically addressed (e.g., $5 + 3$, $6 + 3$). Although flexibility of strategies is addressed throughout the program, the final pieces of the teaching sequence focus on different ways students might use known facts to find an unknown fact. Discussions that show flexibility are critical to expanding students' thinking about numbers and the many ways they can be joined or separated. These students share their thoughts about finding the sum of $5 + 3$:

"$5 + 2 = 7$ and it's just 1 more, so $5 + 3 = 8$."

"If you double 3 it's 6, and 5 is 2 more than 3, so $5 + 3 = 8$."

"$7 + 3 = 10$, so $5 + 3 = 8$ because it's 2 less than 10."

There is more than one way to think about joining numbers. These comments demonstrate students' strategic reasoning and their enhanced understanding of numbers.

Connecting new facts to previously discussed number concepts allows students to continually build mastery of addition and subtraction basic facts. Figure 1 outlines a brief rationale for the sequence in which the facts are introduced within this book. We recognize, however, that students and instructional programs differ and that teachers might choose, or be required, to introduce facts in a different sequence. Although we believe that there is strong justification for this sequence, we have carefully developed strategies and activities that support instruction of math facts even if the order in which you present the facts differs from the sequence described below.

The lessons and activities in this book focus on strengthening students' number concepts to support their mastery of basic math facts. Teachers who have a deep understanding of big ideas related to numbers and the ways in

Foundation Facts	
+1/+2	Students build on their understanding of counting by exploring 1 or 2 more and 1 or 2 less.
+0	Using their knowledge of the concept of addition, students explore what happens when they add or subtract nothing from a quantity.
+10	Adding 10 to a single-digit number results in a 2-digit sum. Students explore adding 10 in order to build understanding and automaticity that will be needed later when exploring the using-ten strategy.
Doubles	Students explore the concept of doubling and what it means to add 2 groups of equal size.
Making Ten	Because 10 is foundational in our number system, students explore the different ways in which 2 addends result in a sum of 10. This knowledge becomes critical as they later explore using tens to find unknown facts.
Building on the Foundation	
Using tens	Now that students know combinations of addends that have a sum of 10, they use their understanding of the flexibility of numbers to find ways to break apart addends to create simpler facts by using tens (e.g., 9 + 7 is changed to 10 + 6).
Using doubles	Students' knowledge of doubles facts is now put to use to find unknown facts that are near-doubles (e.g., 4 + 5 might be thought of as 4 + 4 + 1).

Figure 1. *This suggested teaching sequence begins with simpler facts and then connects each new set of facts to students' previous experiences.*

which those big ideas relate to the teaching of math facts, and who have developed a repertoire of instructional techniques and classroom activities to highlight those big ideas, are able to simplify the task of mastering basic math facts for their students.

Why are activities and resources on a CD?

Along with the many easy-to-implement student activities described within the book, you will find a teacher-friendly CD filled with customizable versions of the activities. Because the CD materials are produced in a Microsoft Word format, you can easily modify the activity pages to make them simpler or more complex, personalize the tasks to insert your students' names or names of familiar places or events, and adapt the activities to work with any set of math facts. On the CD, you will find the featured activities (described within the book) for each set of facts as well as some additional activities, often modified from a featured activity for a different set of facts, to provide a multitude of practice tasks from which you can choose. The CD also includes teacher tools (e.g., hundred charts, addition tables, assessments, and game templates) to simplify your planning and reduce your preparation time.

Resource for Professional Learning Communities

Effective teachers constantly reflect on their own teaching. They gather new ideas, try them with students, reflect on their successes, and find ways to continually refine their teaching. At the conclusion of this book, questions are posed to stimulate reflection about the key points within the chapters. These guiding questions are designed for your personal reflection or for use in school-based study groups. Discussion about math facts instruction within our professional learning communities broadens our understanding and improves our teaching.

Our Goal

The purpose of this book is to explore ways to support all students in mastering addition and subtraction facts. By focusing on big ideas, strengthening students' understanding of math operations, developing strategic thinking, and providing varied and engaging practice tasks to promote fluency, our students will be better equipped to both understand math facts and commit the facts to memory. Whether you are introducing students to basic facts, reviewing facts, or providing remediation for struggling students, this book provides you with insights and activities to simplify this complex and vital component of math teaching.

CHAPTER ONE

Understanding Addition and Subtraction

It is essential to build an understanding of the concepts of addition and subtraction prior to asking students to memorize addition and related subtraction facts. Students who understand the concepts of addition and subtraction are able to understand the connections between math facts and real situations (i.e., the flowers in a vase with 2 daisies and 9 roses are represented by 2 + 9). These students are better equipped to effectively solve math problems by choosing the operation that makes sense (i.e., "If you put together the daisies and roses, you get how many flowers are in the vase altogether, so you have to add 2 + 9 to find that out."). They are better

able to make reasonable judgments about sums and differences (i.e., "It's a little more than 10 because $2 + 8 = 10$."). And students who understand the concepts of addition and subtraction are better prepared to begin the task of memorizing math facts because they understand what they are being asked to memorize.

Exploring Big Ideas to Develop Math Fact Strategies

Big ideas are essential to the development of understanding (Wiggins and McTighe 1998). Without big ideas to hold them together, math facts are just isolated bits of knowledge. It is the big ideas about numbers that help students make sense of math facts. These ideas form the foundation for the development of math fact strategies. The following big ideas are at the center of math fact teaching.

Our number system is a system of patterns.

Once students understand that our number system is a system of patterns, they begin to recognize patterns in math facts that will help them make sense of, and remember, the facts. Noticing the patterns that emerge when observing the equations $6 + 4 = 10$, $7 + 3 = 10$, $8 + 2 = 10$, and $9 + 1 = 10$ will lead to some interesting discussions as students attempt to explain their observations. Our number system is a system of patterns, and these patterns emerge throughout the exploration of addition and subtraction facts. Because of these patterns, math facts are predictable.

The order of the factors does not change the sum (the commutative property).

As a student visualizes placing 2 green pencils and 3 red pencils in her pencil box, it doesn't matter if she thinks about $2 + 3$ or $3 + 2$, there are still 5 pencils in the pencil box. Investigations begin to confirm the commutative (order) property, and when students' experiences convince them that the order of the factors does not change the sum, the task of memorizing math facts is immediately simplified by the realization that only half as many facts need to be committed to memory (i.e., if they know the sum of $3 + 5$, then they also know the sum of $5 + 3$).

Addition and subtraction are inverse operations.

There is a connection between the operations of addition and subtraction. Addition and subtraction are inverse operations. We can undo the action of one by performing the other operation. Fact families are often explored to highlight this connection (e.g., $3 + 7 = 10$; $7 + 3 = 10$; $10 - 7 = 3$; $10 - 3 = 7$). Fact families are powerful ways to support students with mastering math facts because recall of one fact results in recall of the other three related facts.

Numbers are flexible. They can be broken apart to more easily perform an operation.

Numbers can be composed and decomposed. We can join several smaller sets to form one large set (e.g., 3 items and 5 items can be joined to make a group of 8 items) or break one set into smaller sets (e.g., 8 can be broken into sets of 3 and 5). Breaking one addend apart, to create a simpler way to perform an operation, allows us to find sums more easily. When faced with finding the sum of $9 + 7$, students might break apart 7 into $1 + 6$ and easily find the sum of $(9 + 1) + 6$, which is simply $10 + 6$. The numbers were quickly decomposed and composed to make the calculation more friendly.

These big ideas about numbers are central to students' understanding and should guide the types of questions that are posed during student explorations or class discussions.

What does each number represent?

What patterns do you notice in the sums and differences?

Does the order of the addends affect the sum? Give examples to justify your thinking.

Do you notice a connection between this addition equation and this subtraction equation?

Can you write a missing-factor addition equation to match the subtraction equation?

Can you break apart one of the addends to more easily find the sum?

Our goal is to continually reinforce the big ideas related to math facts as we help students develop addition and subtraction strategies.

Building Understanding Prior to Focusing on Fluency

Initial experiences with addition and subtraction are designed to help students understand the mathematical process, as well as its symbolic representation. It is important that students attach meaning to the operations before there is any focus on fact fluency. Guided investigations using manipulatives, acting out addition and subtraction scenarios, and exploring the operations through problem-based experiences and literature-related tasks help students gain insights about the operations and grasp the new concepts.

Exploring Symbolic Representations Understanding the big idea that equations are simply symbolic representations of situations is a foundational understanding. Consistently recording addition and subtraction equations, as students explore the concepts using manipulatives, helps our students begin to understand what the numbers and symbols represent. Asking probing questions to focus students on the meaning of the numbers within the equations is also helpful.

What does the 3 represent?

What does the 4 represent?

What does that symbol tell us?

Using Models to Represent Addition and Subtraction

Our students' understanding is deepened when they can visualize the addition and subtraction processes. Often, teachers engage students in acting out addition or subtraction scenarios or modeling the processes on a whiteboard, an overhead, or a document camera. We encourage students to create their own visuals for addition and subtraction processes through their drawings or explorations with manipulatives. Each time students visualize the processes, they become increasingly familiar with the meaning behind these operations. Number lines, ten-frames, number charts, and modeling with manipulatives all create visual representations of addition and subtraction and should be integrated frequently into math facts lessons.

Number Lines to Represent Addition and Subtraction

Students begin using number lines as they explore counting. They see the counting numbers increase as they move to the right on the number line and decrease as they move to the left. As the concept of addition is introduced, students can rely on this familiar tool to visualize adding 1 more (moving to the right) or subtracting 1 (moving to the left). Students quickly recognize that each jump to the right on the number line represents adding 1 more and each jump to the left represents 1 less.

Initial number line experiences for addition might include jumping on a floor-sized number line or jumping a cube or counter on a desk-sized number strip (see CD). Consistently recording the corresponding equation will help students connect the abstract representation to their concrete experiences.

Number lines clearly illustrate the commutative property (see Figure 1.1), helping students see that the order of the addends will not affect the sum. As students show 3 jumps followed by 2 jumps to land on 5, and then show 2 jumps followed by 3 jumps to still land on 5, they are visualizing this important property. Students can use double number lines to

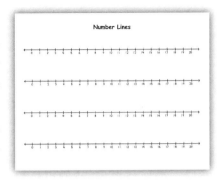

Tip Models build understanding of the commutative property. When students understand this property, the process of mastering math facts is simplified.

Figure 1.1 *Using number lines to represent math facts helps students grasp the commutative property.*

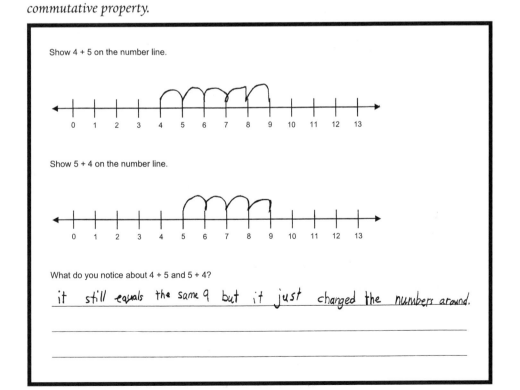

Show 4 + 5 on the number line.

0 1 2 3 4 5 6 7 8 9 10 11 12 13

Show 5 + 4 on the number line.

0 1 2 3 4 5 6 7 8 9 10 11 12 13

What do you notice about 4 + 5 and 5 + 4?

it still equals the same 9 but it just changed the numbers around.

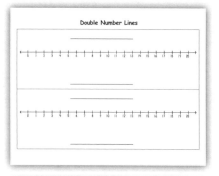

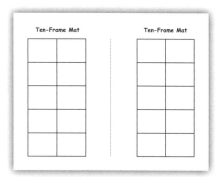

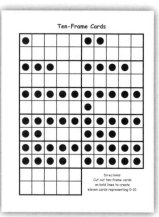

explore this property (see CD) by recording the equations, with addends in different orders, and showing the jumps on the top and bottom of their double number line. Seeing is believing!

Using Manipulatives to Represent Addition and Subtraction

Real materials (e.g., raisins, buttons, beans) or manipulatives (e.g., counters, cubes, square tiles) can be arranged and manipulated to represent the actions of addition or subtraction. Using a part-part-whole work mat (see the CD), students place 3 red buttons in one *part* and 5 blue buttons in the other *part*, and then move the 8 buttons to show the *whole*. Or simply placing 2 beans on one side of their desk and 3 beans on the other side of their desk, and then moving the beans together to make a group of 5 beans in the center of their desks, shows the joining action of addition. Drawing a large circle on construction paper, or forming a circle from tied string, and then placing 9 raisins in the circle and removing 4 raisins, shows the take-away, or separating, action of subtraction. Or lining sets of tiles in rows side by side to see how many more might be in one set creates a comparison model of subtraction. Using manipulatives to show the actions of these operations strengthens students' understanding.

Investigations with models also serve to prove the commutative property. Rather than memorizing this property, student explorations demonstrate that the order of the addends does not affect the product. The students in Figure 1.2 created chains to represent 5 + 3 and 3 + 5, finding they had the same total number of links.

Drawing models of addition and subtraction is also an effective way to focus attention on the commutative property. As students draw 2 red lollipops and 4 green lollipops, or switch it to 4 red lollipops and 2 green lollipops, they begin to notice that the total number of lollipops is the same. Encouraging students to observe, discuss, and make conjectures based on their drawings leads them to the conclusion that the order of the factors does not affect the product.

Ten-Frames to Represent Addition and Subtraction

Ten-frame templates (see CD) allow students to quickly visualize 10, making them a handy tool for investigations about addition and subtraction. Students might select a small ten-frame card (see CD) and determine the quantity of dots on the card and the quantity of dots that must be added to get 10. Students might place counters in sections of a ten-frame template and investigate how many more counters might be needed to make ten. Students might

Figure 1.2 *These students create chains for addition facts, noticing that the order of the addends does not change the sum.*

explore subtraction by beginning with all 10 sections filled with counters and then removing some. Do they know how many are left? Ten-frames create an effective visual for the addition and subtraction process, as well as provide repeated practice with facts that make ten, knowledge of which is a critical step in achieving math fact mastery.

Again, as our students actively explore with ten-frames, insights occur. "If I have 10 and remove 4, I get 6. And if I have 10 and remove 6, I get 4!" These insights continue to expand our students' understanding of numbers and properties.

Number Charts to Represent Addition and Subtraction

When investigating basic facts, a twenty chart (see CD) is a useful and familiar tool for visualizing addition and subtraction processes. It is similar to a hundred chart and allows students to view the progression of numbers in the counting sequence, but limits the amount of numbers that students examine. Students might place counters on numbers, or circle the numbers, as they explore addends. As students explore 2 + 10 and 5 + 10 and 7 + 10, they notice that the sum appears directly below the

Twenty Chart

1	2	3	4	5	6	7	8	9	10
11	12	13	14	15	16	17	18	19	20

Twenty Chart

1	2	3	4	5	6	7	8	9	10
11	12	13	14	15	16	17	18	19	20

Twenty Chart

1	2	3	4	5	6	7	8	9	10
11	12	13	14	15	16	17	18	19	20

1	2	3	4	5	6	7	8	9	10
11	12	13	14	15	16	17	18	19	20

Figure 1.3 *A 1–20 chart allows students to visualize the pattern created when adding 10 to any single-digit number.*

first addend as in Figure 1.3. Adding 10 to any single-digit number becomes an easy task with this insight.

Exploring the Addition Table   Addition tables (see CD) are valuable tools that allow students to locate answers to unknown facts, explore patterns, and even track their progress by shading their known facts. Primary students benefit from an introduction to the addition table. Some students may confuse the table with a hundred chart, others may not understand the use of rows and columns to locate sums, and still others may not understand that the outer row and column are addends and the inner sections represent sums. Spend some time helping your students get comfortable with the addition table.

- Enlarge a blank table and complete it with your class by recording the sums as you address each set of facts.

- Use a straight edge to highlight rows and columns as you help students better understand the organization of the chart.

- Use colored transparent plastic strips to cover a row and column to help students visualize where the two intersect to locate the sum.

- Record the addends in the top row and left column in a different color than the sums to distinguish them from the sums.

Take the time to familiarize your students with this critical tool so they are better able to understand the data it contains and effectively use it as they work toward math fact mastery.

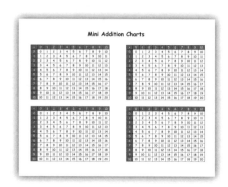

Exploring the Concepts of Addition and Subtraction Through Problems

Exploring addition and subtraction through problem-based contexts builds an understanding of the operations. Throughout the book, many student explorations will be set in problem contexts to ensure that students are developing conceptual understanding as they move toward fluency. Providing students with opportunities to engage in problem tasks has multiple benefits including the development of mathematical reasoning, opportunities to communicate mathematical thinking, ongoing practice with specific sets of math facts, and the enthusiasm that is generated by interesting problems.

Classifying Addition and Subtraction Problems

There are four categories of problems that classify the action of the operations of addition and subtraction: join, separate, part-part-whole, and compare (Carpenter et al. 1999). Explorations with word problems, in which students act out, model, and discuss situations, are critical for building understanding of these problem types. Exploring problem situations and recording the corresponding equations helps students develop meaning for the operations and helps them see the connection to math facts.

Join
$5 + 3 = 8$

- John took some pennies out of his piggy bank. He found 3 more pennies. He had 8 pennies altogether. How many did John take out of his piggy bank? ($n + 3 = 8$; initial quantity unknown)

- John took 5 pennies out of his piggy bank. He found some more pennies. He had 8 pennies altogether. How many pennies did John find? ($5 + n = 8$; change unknown)

- John took 5 pennies out of his piggy bank. He found 3 more pennies. How many pennies did he have altogether? ($5 + 3 = n$; result unknown)

Separate
$9 - 3 = 6$

- Ellen baked some cupcakes. She ate 3 of them. She had 6 cupcakes left. How many did she bake? ($n - 3 = 6$; initial quantity unknown)

- Ellen baked 9 cupcakes. She ate some. She had 6 left. How many did she eat? ($9 - n = 6$; change unknown)

- Ellen baked 9 cupcakes. She ate 3 of them. How many did she have left? ($9 - 3 = n$; result unknown)

Part-Part-Whole
5 + 7 = 12

- Kristen had a vase filled with 12 flowers. 5 flowers were red and the rest were yellow. How many flowers were yellow? ($5 + n = 12$; part unknown)

- Kristen had a vase of flowers. 5 of the flowers were red and 7 were yellow. How many flowers were in Kristen's vase? ($5 + 7 = n$; whole unknown)

Compare
7 − 4 = 3

- Oscar had 7 balloons. Deryn had 4 blue balloons. How many more balloons did Oscar have? ($7 - 4 = n$ or $4 + n = 7$; difference unknown)

- Oscar had 7 balloons. Deryn had 3 fewer balloons than Oscar. How many balloons did Deryn have? ($7 - 3 = n$ or $3 + n = 7$; quantity unknown)

- Deryn had 4 balloons. Oscar had 3 more balloons than Deryn. How many balloons did Oscar have? ($4 + 3 = n$ or $n - 4 = 3$; larger quantity unknown)

Tip **Writing and Drawing Story Problems**

Asking students to write their own problems for math facts provides a solid assessment of their understanding of the expressions. Students might be assigned a fact and asked to draw a picture to show the fact or might randomly select a fact card and draw a picture or write a story problem to match the fact on the card (see Figure 1.4).

Figure 1.4 *This student creates a drawing of 6 + 2 to show her understanding of the fact.*

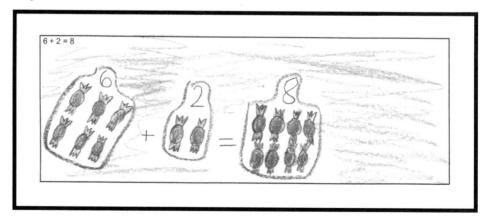

Our focus is on understanding the situation presented in a problem rather than simply teaching students to rely on key words. Although words like *altogether*, *left*, or *how many more* can be helpful in providing a clue to the action in the problem, they can also be misleading or do not appear in some problems. Students who rely solely on words, rather than understanding, often find themselves confused when faced with problem tasks.

Exploring Operations Through Children's Literature

When reading or listening to stories, followed by discussions of the math situations represented in the stories, our students experience addition and subtraction in a context that makes sense to them. In *Rooster's Off to See the World* by Eric Carle (1972), Rooster is joined by his friends on a trip to see the world. As each group of friends joins him, students experience the concept of addition. When the sun goes down, some friends decide to go home, and the concept of subtraction becomes real. *Animals on Board*, by Stuart J. Murphy (1998), shares the story of trucker Jill who sees, and adds, truckloads of animals as they pass her along the road. In *Elevator Magic* by Stuart J. Murphy (1997), Ben pushes the buttons in the elevator as he and his Mom make their way to the ground floor, providing a fun context and an effective visual of the subtraction process.

In the following chapters, you will notice many lesson suggestions that focus on a rich piece of children's literature. These are highlighted throughout the book as Literature Links. Some stories have a clear connection to a specific fact strategy, and others offer examples of how children's literature can be used to set contexts for mathematics investigations. A resource list of all titles is located in the References.

To make the most of the integration of this literature into math facts lessons, a "before, during, after" approach is presented. *Before* reading the story, the context is set for the story, prior knowledge is assessed, or a question is posed to guide students' thinking as they listen to the story. *During* reading, students might be asked to make predictions or the story might be reread as students act out the events using manipulatives. *After* reading, the concepts are further explored through investigations, problems, and discussions. The stories engage students, set a context for further explorations, and provide a memorable lesson related to the math facts being studied.

Ongoing Reference to the Concepts   As students go through the school day, there are many opportunities to reinforce the concept of addition and make connections between addition and subtraction. Teachers who consistently refer to addition or subtraction scenarios provide repeated exposure to the concepts. Capitalize on everyday examples to build students' understanding of the operations.

4 chairs are at 1 table and 3 chairs are at another table, or a student removes a chair from a table with 5 chairs.

10 students want chocolate milk and 5 students want white milk.

5 pencils are red and 6 pencils are blue.

On the calendar, tomorrow is 1 day after today (+1) and yesterday was 1 day before today (−1).

Partner Explorations

Providing students with many opportunities to explore addition and subtraction through games and investigations will help them further develop their understanding. Activities, like the following, that are simple but provide visual experiences and opportunities for partner discussions are optimal.

Circle Circle

Have partners draw two circles on a large piece of construction paper. Provide them with a 1–6 number cube or die, 12 counters, and a paper to record number sentences. Have one student roll and place that quantity of counters in one circle. Then, the other partner rolls and places that number of counters in the other circle. Students work together to write an addition number sentence to show the total number of counters.

A variation of *Circle Circle* might be for students to draw pictures to represent the facts, rather than using manipulatives. Partners draw two circles, each player rolls the number cube and draws that number of stars or smiley faces inside a circle, then students work together to find the sum and record the number sentence.

Ways to Make Six

Provide students with 6 two-color counters, a cup, and a blank sheet of paper. Have them fold the paper in half and draw a red circle on the top of one half and a yellow circle on the top of the other half. Have them gently spill the counters onto the table and record the number of red in the column with the red circle and the number of yellow in the column with the yellow circle. Challenge students to find different ways they can make 6 (or any sum).

Capture and Count

Provide students with a set of 10 cubes and a paper cup. Have one partner pick up some cubes and place them on her desk. The players count the total number of cubes. The other partner then captures (covers) some, but not all, of the cubes with the paper cup. The players count the number of cubes they can still see (not covered by the cup) and work together to figure out how many are under the cup.

The Classroom Environment

Students are supported in understanding math facts when the classroom contains cues to the meaning of the operations. Interactive bulletin boards, word walls, and centers provide opportunities for ongoing exposure to addition and subtraction concepts.

Interactive Bulletin Boards

Interactive bulletin boards can be both an instructional tool as well as an ongoing reminder of addition and subtraction concepts. Record a math fact on an index card or sentence strip, then "show the fact" through the bulletin board illustration. For 3 + 4, post 3 happy jack-o'-lanterns and 4 scary ones. Students can become actively involved by brainstorming and writing a class story problem to post on the board. "There were 3 happy jack-o'-lanterns and 4 scary ones. How many were there altogether?" Change the facts by adding or removing jack-o'-lanterns, then challenge students to revise the story problems. Simple illustrations (e.g., blue and green balloons, yellow and red lollipops, dogs and cats, boy gingerbread men and girl gingerbread men, pink hearts and red hearts) can easily set a context for addition and subtraction facts.

Word Walls

Understanding of math ideas is enhanced when students understand the language being used in math class. Students benefit from an introduction, and repeated exposure, to the vocabulary of addition and subtraction. Using synonyms, pictures, and examples when we introduce new words enhances our students' understanding. Posting words on a class word wall allows students to frequently refer to the wall as they process the vocabulary. Adding visuals to your word wall (e.g., pictures, symbols, or equations) offers helpful clues to the meaning of the words.

Words on your wall should be written large enough for everyone in the classroom to see them. Having sentence strips and a thick black marker within reach allows you to quickly record a word that comes up in classroom conversations and immediately add it to your wall. Consider including the following words:

part	*whole*	*add*	*subtract*
plus	*minus*	*in all*	*left*
compare	*sum*	*difference*	*join*
more	*equal*		

Some of these words are commonly thought of as cues, or keys, to choosing the appropriate operation to solve a problem, but our goal is for students to understand the meaning of these words, not simply identify them as key words. Often these words are aligned with a specific operation, but not always. Understanding is more powerful than simple association. For example, *left* is typically thought of as a cue to subtract, but consider the following problem:

> There were 3 jackets left on the playground on Monday. There were 4 jackets left on the playground on Tuesday. How many jackets were left on the playground?

Would your students immediately see the word *left* and subtract to find the solution, even though the problem clearly illustrates a *joining* process? An understanding of words, coupled with an understanding of operations, is essential for our students to truly grasp addition and subtraction processes and problems.

Centers

Classroom centers provide a wonderful opportunity for repeated exposure to addition and subtraction concepts. A Math Literature Center, in which students read math-related literature containing addition and subtraction scenarios, allows students to develop deeper understandings. A Block/Manipulative Center, in which students use concrete materials to represent math facts, allows students to explore the concepts in a hands-on way. Students might use stamps or stickers or simply draw pictures to represent math facts in a Math Art Center, or visit a Math Games Center to practice math facts while playing one of the many games presented throughout this book. Simple activities make effective center tasks, as the goal is simply to provide exploration and repetition with math facts.

Beginning with Understanding

Automaticity with math facts is our goal, but before any math fact fluency practice begins, understanding of the operations is essential. Through investigations, discussions, visual models, stories, and hands-on explorations, students develop an understanding of the concepts of addition and subtraction and are then ready to begin to commit those facts to memory.

CHAPTER TWO

Plus 1 and Plus 2

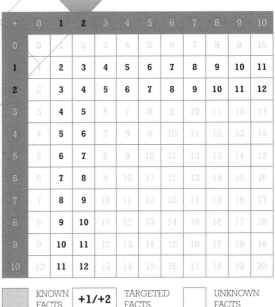

+	0	1	2	3	4	5	6	7	8	9	10
0	0	1	2	3	4	5	6	7	8	9	10
1	1	2	3	4	5	6	7	8	9	10	11
2	2	3	4	5	6	7	8	9	10	11	12
3	3	4	5	6	7	8	9	10	11	12	13
4	4	5	6	7	8	9	10	11	12	13	14
5	5	6	7	8	9	10	11	12	13	14	15
6	6	7	8	9	10	11	12	13	14	15	16
7	7	8	9	10	11	12	13	14	15	16	17
8	8	9	10	11	12	13	14	15	16	17	18
9	9	10	11	12	13	14	15	16	17	18	19
10	10	11	12	13	14	15	16	17	18	19	20

KNOWN FACTS   +1/+2 TARGETED FACTS   UNKNOWN FACTS

As we begin our focus on mastery of addition and subtraction math facts, we consider our students' current math skills and understandings and explore ways to build on those skills. Our students can count groups of objects and have developed an understanding of one-to-one correspondence. We have introduced them to the concepts of addition and subtraction and have given them opportunities to explore these concepts through various models and problem situations. As our students begin to understand addition as a total, a whole, or

a joined amount, they are able to find sums in concrete ways, using manipulatives to represent items, physically moving the items together, and then counting all of them to find the total. Although this will lead them to the correct sum and it reveals an understanding of the addition process, it is certainly not the most efficient way for students to determine the total number of objects. It is time to build on our students' beginning understanding of addition and subtraction by targeting specific sets of facts and focusing on strategies that allow them to efficiently add without counting every object. Our goal is to provide students with multiple strategies to quickly and efficiently find sums and differences. This focus on strategies serves to expand their understanding of numbers and properties.

Knowing that many students are at a *counting all* stage of addition, we begin our math facts strategy teaching with a focus on +1 and +2. Building on students' understanding of counting and their previous experiences with number lines, we begin to transition students from counting all to beginning with one addend and counting on (or counting back for subtraction) to find the sum (or difference). Because of the simplicity of counting 1 or 2 more, or 1 or 2 less, the perfect place to begin our journey for math fact understanding and automaticity is with +1/+2 and −1/−2 facts!

Focusing on the Big Ideas

Exploring big ideas about mathematics provides the backdrop for our exploration of 1 more, 2 more, 1 less, and 2 less. Some big ideas follow.

The sum when 1 is added to a quantity is the next counting number.

Adding 1 to a quantity is simply counting 1 more number in our counting sequence. Students' experiences with number lines provide them with a helpful visual for recognizing this big idea. In the same way, adding 2 is simply counting 2 more numbers in our counting sequence. When transitioning to subtraction, students connect this idea to counting backward, or moving from right to left on a number line. Students' ability to count from 1–12 both forward and backward is a prerequisite skill for +1/+2 thinking.

Our number system is a system of patterns.

Noticing that adding 1 or 2, or subtracting 1 or 2, is simply moving 1 or 2 places in our counting sequence gives order to math facts. Seeing this on number lines or number charts and connecting the idea to their counting experiences help students recognize the predictability of math facts. Math facts make sense.

Addition is a joining or combining process.

When we add, we are joining objects or combining parts to find a whole. The expression 6 + 1 represents joining 6 objects and 1 object to find the quantity of the new set, the combined amount. When focusing on math facts, this understanding helps students assess the reasonableness of their answers.

Subtraction is a separation or comparison process.

When we subtract, we are separating objects from a whole set (taking away) or comparing sets of objects to find the difference. The expression 6 − 1 might represent 1 apple being removed from a basket of 6 apples or might represent a comparison between a set of 6 yellow apples and 1 red apple to find out how many more or less are in 1 set. When focusing on math facts, this understanding helps students assess the reasonableness of their answers.

The order of the addends does not change the sum (the commutative property).

Whether students are visualizing 5 balloons added to 1 balloon (5 + 1) or 1 balloon added to 5 balloons (1 + 5), they will notice that the sum is the same. This knowledge immediately simplifies math fact mastery. As students explore 3 + 1 and 5 + 1 and 8 + 1 by simply adding 1 more, or finding the next counting number, they recognize that they also know 1 + 3 and 1 + 5 and 1 + 8 because the order of the addends does not matter. Any time students see 1 or 2 as an addend, they learn to begin with the larger addend and then simply add 1 or 2.

Addition and subtraction are inverse processes.

There is a natural connection between the operations of addition and subtraction because of the connection between the joining and separating process or the part-part-whole concept. If we join a set of 3 cubes and a set of 2 cubes to form a new set with a total of 5 cubes, it also makes sense that if we take that set of 5 cubes and remove 2 cubes, we will have 3 cubes remaining. Fact families highlight this connection (e.g., 3 + 1 = 4; 1 + 3 = 4; 4 − 1 = 3; 4 − 3 = 1). When working on automaticity with both addition and subtraction facts, we develop addition strategies, provide repeated practice for fluency with addition facts, explore subtraction concepts, and emphasize the connection between addition and subtraction. In this way, students use their knowledge of addition facts to develop fluency with related subtraction facts.

Key questions related to the big ideas for +1, +2 facts are:

When you add 1, how do you know what the sum will be? Explain your thinking.

When you add 2, how do you know what the sum will be? Explain your thinking.

Does the order of the addends change the sum? Give examples to justify your thinking.

How might a number line (or number chart) help you with +1 and +2 facts?

How do you know when your answer makes sense?

What is 30 + 1? Explain how you know.

What might be a quick way to find a −1/−2 fact?

How might you use a number line (or number chart) to find a −1/−2 fact?

If you don't know a subtraction fact, how might knowing addition facts help you?

Our goal is to continually reinforce the big ideas related to math facts as we help students develop addition and subtraction strategies.

Understanding +1, +2 Facts

Literature Link: *Mouse Count*

Students are better able to make sense of abstract ideas when those ideas are set in a context that makes sense to them. Literature provides an engaging context for the study of math facts. In *Mouse Count* (1991) by Ellen Stoll Walsh, 10 clever mice escape a greedy snake that is planning to eat them for dinner. The story sets a context for exploring *counting on* as a strategy for adding 1 or 2.

Before Reading Show students the cover illustration. Ask them to turn to a partner and tell what they think the book will be about. Have a few students share their ideas with the class. Ask students if mice and snakes get along. Have students tell a partner what they would do if they were a mouse and they saw a snake. Tell them you will be reading *Mouse Count* to see what these mice did.

During Reading Have students count along with you as mice are added to the jar.

After Reading   Begin an investigation to explore 1 more and 2 more. Copy the mice templates (see CD) on card stock and place them in small plastic bags to represent mice in the snake's jar, placing different amounts of mice (1–10) in each bag. Provide students with a *Mice in a Jar* recording sheet (see CD) or plain paper to record their data, and 2 additional mice to use as they explore adding 1 or adding 2 to their jars (bags) of mice. As snakes, students work with partners to choose a bag and count the number of mice in the bag. After counting the number of mice, students find the total if 1 mouse is added to their bag. Students then record the new number of mice on their recording sheet, write an addition number sentence to represent adding 1 mouse to the bag, and draw a picture to show what they have done, as in Figure 2.1. Then, students add a second mouse to the bag and find the total if 2 mice are added

Figure 2.1 *This student explores adding 1 and 2 mice to the jar.*

Mice in a Jar

In bag __B__ there were __3__ mice.

I added 1 mouse so there were ___4___.

I added 2 mice and there were ___5___.

Draw a picture and write a number sentence to show how many mice there were when you added 1 mouse to the bag.

$$3 + 1 = 4$$

Draw a picture and write a number sentence to show how many mice there were when you added 2 mice to the bag.

$$3 + 2 = 5$$

to the original number of mice in the bag. Students record the new quantity of mice, their addition number sentence, and draw a picture to represent adding 2 mice to the original bag. Labeling bags with *A*, *B*, *C*, and so on for each different quantity (e.g., bag A has 1 mouse, bag B has 2 mice, etc.) will allow you to assess students' accuracy when you collect and review their recording sheets.

After students investigate and record their data about adding mice to a couple different bags (note that they will need a new recording sheet for each bag), have partners share their results with the class. Create a chart on the board, overhead, or on chart paper, like in Figure 2.2, to record the class' findings. To begin the sharing, ask students to tell you the fewest mice that were in a jar. Because 1 mouse was the fewest you placed in a jar, start with that number as you record their data on your class chart. Ask partners who explored the bag containing 1 mouse to share how many mice were in the jar after they added 1 more. Record the number sentence on the chart (e.g., *1 + 1 = 2*), thinking aloud as you record (e.g., "So you started with 1 mouse and then you added 1 mouse and you had 2 altogether, so 1 mouse plus 1 mouse equals 2 mice, so I'll write *1 + 1 = 2*."). Do the same for adding 2 mice to the bag, recording *1 + 2 = 3* and verbalizing why that number sentence makes sense. Have students share their data to complete the chart, moving in order from a bag with 1 mouse to a bag with 2 mice, 3 mice, and so on. Recording the data in an organized way, from 1–10 mice in the bags, allows patterns to emerge on your class chart. Ask students to discuss the chart with their partners, posing questions like the following.

What do you notice about the different number sentences on our chart?

Do you notice any patterns as you look across the rows?

Do you notice any patterns as you look down the columns?

Discuss students' observations, which will likely include:

The numbers go in order like 1, 2, 3, 4, 5 or 2, 3, 4, 5, 6.

There is always 1 more in the +1 column because we added 1 more mouse.

The +2 column is one more than the +1 column because we added one then we added another 1.

It's just like counting 1 more when we add 1.

Number of Mice in Bag	Plus 1 Mouse	Plus 2 Mice
1	1 + 1 = 2	1 + 2 = 3
2	2 + 1 = 3	2 + 2 = 4
3	3 + 1 = 4	3 + 2 = 5
4	4 + 1 = 5	4 + 2 = 6
5	5 + 1 = 6	5 + 2 = 7
6	6 + 1 = 7	6 + 2 = 8
7	7 + 1 = 8	7 + 2 = 9
8	8 + 1 = 9	8 + 2 = 10
9	9 + 1 = 10	9 + 2 = 11
10	10 + 1 = 11	10 + 2 = 12

Figure 2.2 *Organize and record data from students' investigations to allow them to see patterns and discover insights about adding 1 and 2.*

Probe students' thinking by asking them to talk or write about their insights (see Figure 2.3). Try the *Thinking About +1, +2* recording sheet on the CD or try these prompts:

> *What happens when we add 1 to a number?*
>
> *What happens when we add 2 to a number?*
>
> *How would you know the total without counting the mice or drawing a picture?*

Have students share their ideas with partners and then with the class. Record some big ideas about adding 1 or 2 on your class chart.

Figure 2.3 *This student shares her insights about adding 1.*

What do you notice about adding 1?

I is all ways the next number

0–12 Desk-Sized Number Strip

Directions: Cut out both strips (0–6 and 7–12). Place the blank square under the 6 and tape the strips together to form a 0–12 number strip.

0	1	2	3	4	5	6
	7	8	9	10	11	12

0	1	2	3	4	5	6
	7	8	9	10	11	12

Exploring the Facts: Number Strips to Visualize 1 More and 2 More

As students begin to explore math fact strategies, it is important to provide experiences in which students visualize the facts using a concrete model, are required to move from concrete/visual experiences to symbolic representations of the facts, and have opportunities to discuss their insights about patterns, numbers, and properties. Number strips, enlarged versions of number lines, are an ideal model for exploring +1 and +2.

Provide each pair of students with a desk-sized 0–12 number strip (see CD) and a cube or counter. Pose the following problems. Have students begin with their counter on 0, then jump their counter to the number that represents the first quantity, and finally jump to the right 1 more or 2 more depending on the problem. Stop and record the addition equation on the board following each scenario.

> Deryn took 5 bites of an apple. Then she took 1 more bite. How many bites did she take?

> Kevin put 7 rocks in the back of his wagon. Then he put 2 more rocks in his wagon. How many rocks were in his wagon?

> Rita jumped 10 times. Then she jumped 1 more time. How many times did she jump?

> Oscar caught 3 fish at the lake. Then he caught 2 more. How many fish did he catch altogether?

> Joe made a tower of 6 blocks. He carefully placed 2 more blocks on his tower. How many blocks were in his tower altogether?

Once students have practiced with the class problems, provide each pair with a set of 1–10 number cards and a +1/+2 spinner. Have students choose a card from a facedown pile, place their counter on that number, and then spin to see if they should add 1 or 2. Once they have moved their counter along their number strip to determine the sum, have them record their addition number sentence. As students work, move through the classroom to assess their understanding. Stop to ask questions to individual students, or pairs of students, to assess their understanding. If struggling students are identified, ask them to join you for an additional guided review of the concept.

Once students have explored +1 and +2 through their spinner investigations and recorded the corresponding number sentences, challenge them to summarize their thinking about adding 1 or 2 by talking with their partners about what they noticed. Try some prompts like:

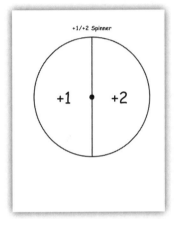

Did the number strip help you add 1 or 2? How?

Do you need the number strip to add 1 or 2?

What if you did not have a number strip, how could you add 1 or 2?

Have partners share some insights with the class, recording some of their thoughts to revisit at the start of tomorrow's lesson.

Supporting All Learners

Some students quickly grasp the concept of 1 more and 2 more, but others may need additional time, and different types of experiences, to develop understanding. The following activities provide additional exposure to +1/+2 facts. They might be used with the whole class or for small teacher-led groups of students who would benefit from further exploration of +1 and +2 facts.

A Fishy +1 Story   *Fish Eyes* by Lois Ehlert (1990) provides a perfect example of +1 thinking. On each page of this counting book, a little fish is seen swimming along with a different group of fish. When you look closely at the margins, you discover that on each page the fish adds himself to the group to discover the new total. Reading the story and stopping to brainstorm and record each +1 equation provide ideal examples of 1 more. To explore *Fish Eyes* in a hands-on way, reread the story and use goldfish crackers or counters to continually add 1 more fish.

Clap, Jump, Wiggle   Many students benefit from movement, so make 1 more and 2 more a kinesthetic experience. Try clapping, hopping, or wiggling 3 times and then 1 more. How many claps or jumps or wiggles did you do? Record the addition equation and try it again.

Hands-on Practice with Pennies   Provide opportunities for students to explore 1 more and 2 more in a hands-on way. Give students a set of 12 pennies and a piggy bank template (see CD). Pose problems like the following.

> John had 4 pennies in his piggy bank. He put 1 more in his bank. How many did he have?

Have students place 4 pennies on their piggy banks, then add 1 more to their banks, and find the total. Ask students to tell, and then write, an addition number sentence to show what happened in the problem. Then, have students clear the piggy bank templates and pose another +1 or +2 problem. After a few problems, begin to ask students to predict the sum before they count to find the sum. Have them explain their predictions. How do they know what 1 more will be?

Exploring the Commutative Property with Manipulatives As we mentioned in Chapter One, a big idea about addition is that the order of the addends does not affect the sum (the commutative property). Students who understand the commutative property will have an easier time memorizing sums simply because they will be memorizing half as many math facts. Exploring this property with manipulatives can help students grasp this big idea. Provide students with manipulatives (e.g., colored counters or cubes). Have them determine the answers to the following questions using their manipulatives.

> Allison had 5 lollipops and 1 peppermint. How many pieces of candy did she have?

> Brendan had 1 lollipop and 5 peppermints. How many pieces of candy did he have?

> Allison won 3 tickets at the arcade. Then she won 2 more. How many did she win altogether?

> Brendan won 2 tickets at the arcade. Then he won 3 more. How many did he win altogether?

Discuss the problems, representing them as addition equations, guiding students to the insight that the order of the factors does not affect the product. Once students get it, suggest that starting with the larger addend and adding 1 or 2 will simplify their recall of the +1/+2 facts.

Check for understanding by asking students to write in their math journals about the following prompt.

> Jimmy says 2 + 3 has a different sum than 3 + 2. Do you agree with him? Why or why not?

The student in Figure 2.4 explains in words and pictures why Jimmy is wrong. Opportunities for students to share their thinking help them process their ideas.

Figure 2.4 *This student's words and pictures are a testament to his understanding of the commutative property.*

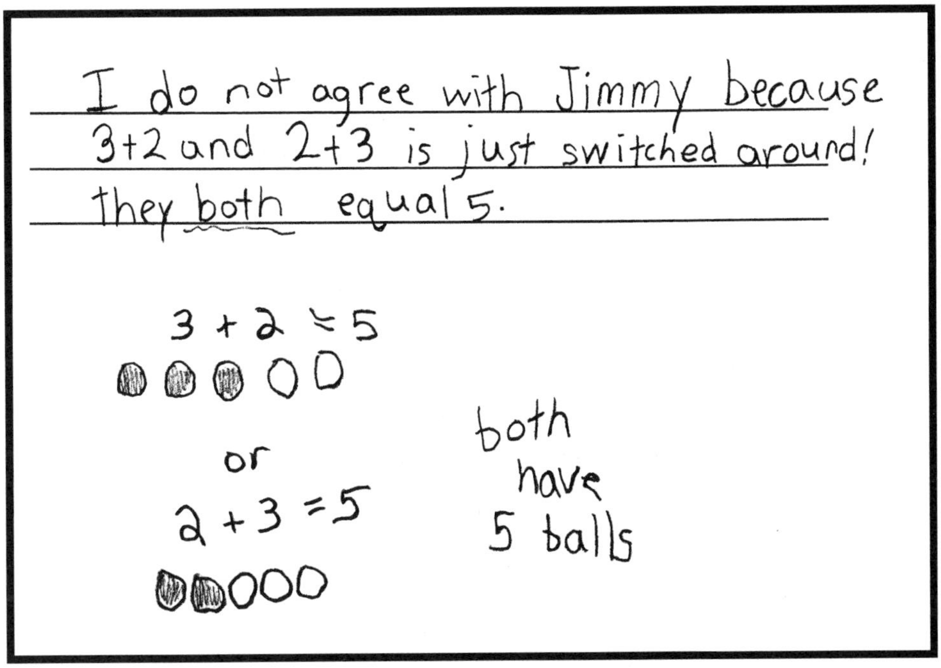

I do not agree with Jimmy because 3+2 and 2+3 is just switched around! they both equal 5.

3 + 2 = 5

or

2 + 3 = 5

both have 5 balls

Building Automaticity

After students have engaged in a variety of activities to understand 1 more and 2 more, it is time to provide them with repeated opportunities to practice the facts. In targeted practice, we are focusing on building automaticity. This practice is short in duration on any given day, but is a routine part of the daily math time.

Tip For quick recall, remind students that when they see a 1 or 2 in an addition math fact, the 1 more, 2 more strategy will simplify it. Regardless of where the 1 or 2 appears in the math fact, it is easiest to start with the larger addend and think *1 more* or *2 more*.

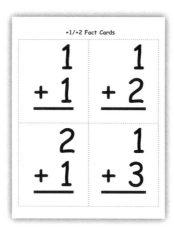

Targeted Practice

Fact Card Practice Fact cards (see CD) can be used for math fact games, center activities, or whole-class reviews. Selecting targeted math facts (e.g., +1/+2 fact cards) and providing short, focused reviews of those facts can be a regular addition to math time; however, rather than having students immediately shout out an answer as in traditional flash card drills, ask students to look at each fact card and think about the sum. When you raise your hand, they may call out each sum or turn and share the sum with a partner. Once students have some experience with the +1/+2 facts, mix in some −1/−2 facts.

Student Fact Card Decks Many teachers like providing students with their own fact card decks. Begin by giving students fact cards for +1/+2 facts. As new facts are introduced, give students the new fact cards to add to their decks. Store the decks in sealable plastic bags, using permanent marker to write students' names on the bags. The fact card bags can be used in class or taken home for additional practice. Templates for student-sized fact cards are provided on the CD.

It may be helpful for some students to color-code their fact cards. To do this, copy student fact card sets and have students lightly shade the cards with a crayon before cutting them apart and storing them in their bags. This can be repeated with a different color each time a new strategy set is introduced.

Tip When focusing on automaticity, consider modifying activities by using just +1 fact cards, allowing students some time to build fluency with those facts, and then adding the +2 fact cards.

Fact Card Jumps Provide students with a set of fact cards for the +1/+2 facts and a *Fact Card Jumps* number line recording sheet (see CD). Have students shuffle the fact cards and select a card. Students then show the fact by creating jumps on the number line (i.e., 4 + 1 is represented by starting at 0 and jumping to 4 and then jumping 1 more place to 5). Have students record the number sentence to go with each number line drawing (see Figure 2.5). Asking them to share insights about adding 1 or 2 allows students to summarize their ideas (see Figure 2.6).

The Value of Games Everyone loves playing games. Beyond the enjoyment, there are many benefits to incorporating games into the math curriculum. Playing games helps students develop number sense and problem-solving skills. Games offer repetition without boredom—students play over and over and still want to keep playing! Capitalize on the benefits of math games by selecting meaningful games for students' math fact practice and by providing ongoing opportunities for them to explore math facts through games.

Figure 2.5 *Representing the math fact on a number line helps this student find the sum.*

Introducing Math Games   To maximize the impact of math fact games, it is wise to model the games with the class before students have the opportunity to play games with partners. Games can be modeled on an overhead, a SMART Board, a whiteboard, or with a document camera to allow students to both see and hear the rules. During modeling, explain the rules and explore possible strategies, or thinking points, for the game. Field questions about the rules of the game or what to do when different situations arise. Have students play the game with partners as you move through the room observing for their understanding of the rules. A thorough introduction to each game will result in smoother play when students are working on their own.

Figure 2.6 *After observing her fact card jumps, this student summarized her insights.*

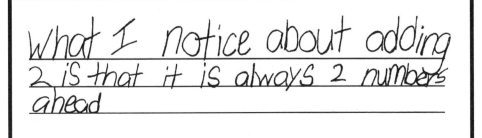

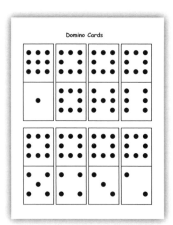

Domino Cards

I Spy 1 More To play *I Spy 1 More*, students need a set of double-nine dominoes for each pair or team. If dominoes are not available, the CD contains templates to create dominoes. Students search for dominoes that have 1 dot on one side (1 more) and write matching addition equations (e.g., a domino with 4 dots on 1 side and 1 dot on the other side is represented by 4 + 1 = 5). Vary the game to play *I Spy 2 More* as students search for dominoes with 2 dots on one side and build related +2 number sentences.

Hop the Line In *Hop the Line*, students are actively involved in jumping a floor-sized 1–12 number line. The number line is created by simply using masking tape for the line, then marking numbers on the tape with magic marker. Each pair needs a number line, 1–10 cards (see CD), a +1/+2 spinner (see CD), and paper to record their equations. Partner 1 selects a number card. Partner 2 jumps along next to the numbers on the number line until she reaches that spot. Partner 1 then spins the spinner and announces whether he is adding 1 or 2. Partner 2 then hops the line to find the sum. She calls out the sum and the players record their number sentence. Players take turns hopping the line.

Dot Card Addition In *Dot Card Addition*, students take turns picking a 1–10 dot card and then spin a +1/+2 spinner (see CD) to determine if they add 1 or add 2. Students record the addition number sentences.

Plus One Two Bingo This adaptation of the traditional game can be played by two or more players and does not require the teacher's participation. In *Plus One Two Bingo*, each student has a 3 × 3 blank bingo grid (see CD). Students write numbers in each of the nine boxes on their grid. Numbers

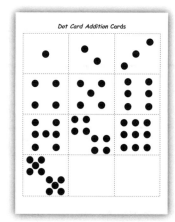

Dot Card Addition Cards

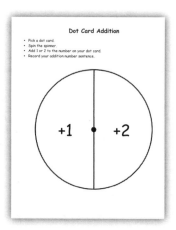

Dot Card Addition
- Pick a dot card.
- Spin the spinner.
- Add 1 or 2 to the number on your dot card.
- Record your addition number sentence.

+1   +2

must be between 2 and 12. The 1–10 cards (see CD) are shuffled and placed in a pile, facedown. One student turns over a card and another spins the +1/+2 spinner (see CD) to see if they should add 1 or add 2 to the number that was picked. Students talk together about the sum and then both students look for it on their grids. If they have it on their grids, they cover it with a bean or marker. If not, they wait until the next number is selected and the spinner is spun and try their luck on the next sum. If a player covers an entire row, column, or diagonal, he has bingo. All players then remove their markers, shuffle the cards, and start again.

Monitoring Progress

Fact Checks   Providing students with frequent opportunities to engage in independent fact reviews provides them with repeated practice, supports fluency, and allows for ongoing monitoring of each student's progress toward automaticity. Fact Checks (see CD), brief worksheet reviews, might focus specifically on the fact being taught (e.g., +1/+2 facts) or might combine previously learned facts. The same worksheet can be done numerous times as students work toward automaticity.

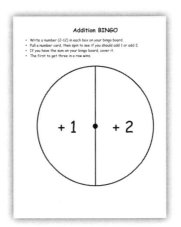

For the first couple of fact sets, sixteen facts appear on each Fact Check. This gives a simpler look to the Fact Check and allows more space for students to record their answers. Two versions of the +1/+2 Fact Check appear on the CD to ensure that all of the facts within the set are addressed. Alternating use of the two versions ensures that students practice all of the facts in the targeted set and allows us to check their knowledge of every fact.

Keep in mind that timed tests can have a negative effect on many students, in particular those students who struggle with memorizing facts. A goal is automaticity, but we want to refrain from comparing one student's time to another's time. Consider using time as a personal motivator by providing a specific amount of time and challenging students to see how many facts they can correctly answer in that amount of time, then further challenge them to "beat their own record" on the following attempt. To track their own progress, students can record the date and the number of math facts answered correctly. These data can be invaluable for student-teacher conferences. The goal of Fact Checks is to identify students' needs so we can provide them with additional instruction or targeted practice. Students who master the facts more quickly should not be rewarded in a way that minimizes the efforts of those students who require more practice to master the skills.

Tip Primary students may have difficulty with fine motor skills, which can impact their ability to quickly record math facts. Consider adjusting the time given for completion of written tasks or allowing students to verbally respond to math Fact Checks.

Connecting to Subtraction

Once students develop an understanding of +1 and +2 facts, take every opportunity to talk about the connection between addition and subtraction facts. Exploring −1 and −2 facts is a natural connection.

Revisiting *Mouse Count*

As students explored +1/+2 with *Mouse Count* by Ellen Stohl Walsh (1991), they investigated the new sums as they added mice. Remind students of the story, or reread the story, and then pose some problems about mice escaping from the jar.

> At the end of the story the jar was filled with 10 mice. What if 1 mouse escaped? How many mice would still be in the jar? What is 1 less than 10?

> If there are 9 mice in the jar and 1 escapes, how many mice would still be in the jar? What is 1 less than 9?

Model a couple scenarios with manipulatives or drawings. Have students use the mice templates to explore the −1 scenarios in a hands-on way. Have students write the subtraction equations to go with their investigations as you record them on the board.

Once students have explored −1 facts, pose scenarios in which 2 mice escape. Have them model with mice templates, make predictions, and record subtraction equations for the −2 problems.

Making Predictions

Counting Crocodiles (1997) by Judy Sierra is a counting book that includes counting from 1–10 as well as counting from 10–1 as a clever monkey counts crocodiles on his travels from an island with lemons to an island with bananas.

Read the book to students, getting them involved in predicting 1 more and 1 less as you read. For the first part of the book, when a specific number of crocodiles is mentioned, stop occasionally to ask students what 1 more would be, then turn the page to confirm their predictions. For the second half of the book, when a specific number of crocodiles is mentioned, have students share how many crocodiles would be 1 less. Turn the page to confirm their predictions. Read the book a second time and record each −1 equation. Particularly for the second part of the story that counts backward, have students share how they came up with their predictions. Can they verbalize what 1 less is and how it relates to counting backward?

Creating 1 Less/2 Less Animal Story Problems

Model writing a −1 or −2 animal story problem. Ask students for the name of an animal (e.g., bear, dog, giraffe) and a number between 2 and 10. If the class decides on 5 giraffes, pose a 1 less or 2 less problem about the giraffes. Could 1 giraffe run off to eat some leaves from a nearby tree? Could 2 giraffes step into the lake to cool off? How many are left? After you've done a few examples of −1/−2 problems, have students work with partners to write word problems that show a −1 or −2 fact as in Figure 2.7. Partners share their problems for the class to solve and you record the math fact as the class solves each problem.

Games and Activities to Promote Fluency

Hop the Line Subtraction   In this modification of the addition activity, students are actively involved in jumping a floor-sized 0–12 number line. The number line is created by simply using masking tape for the line, then marking numbers on the tape with magic marker. Each pair needs a number line, a set of 2–12 number cards, and a −1/−2 spinner (see CD), and paper to record their equations. Partner 1 selects a number card. Partner 2 jumps to that spot on the number line. Partner 1 then spins the spinner and announces whether she is subtracting 1 or 2. Partner 2 then hops the line to find the difference. He calls out the difference and the players record their number sentence. Players take turns hopping the line.

Less Than the Ten-frame   Show a ten-frame card (see CD) and ask students to turn to a partner and share (1) how many dots are on the card and (2) 1 less than the number of dots they saw. Have them record the equation on paper or in their math journals. Challenge students to find 2 less than the number of dots on the card.

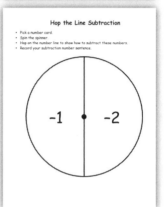

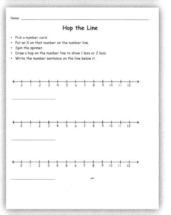

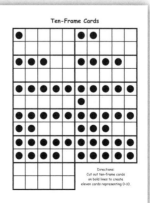

Figure 2.7 *Through this animal story problem, and illustration, this student demonstrates her understanding of 5 − 2.*

There were 5 lions on a rock.
2 lions went to hunt How many
lions were left on the rock.

5−2=3

two hunting

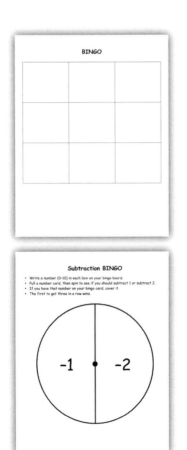

BINGO

Subtraction BINGO

- Write a number (0–10) in each box on your bingo board.
- Pull a number card, then spin to see if you should subtract 1 or subtract 2.
- If you have that number on your bingo card, cover it.
- The first to get three in a row wins.

−1   −2

Minus One Two Bingo   In *Minus One Two Bingo*, each student has a 3 × 3 blank bingo grid (see CD). Students write numbers in each of the nine boxes on their grid. Numbers must be between 0 and 10. The 2–12 number cards are shuffled and placed in a pile, facedown. One student turns over a card and another spins the spinner to see if he should subtract 1 or subtract 2 from the number that was picked. Students talk together to find the difference and then both students look for it on their grids. If they have it on their grids, they cover it with a bean or marker. If not, they wait until the next number is selected and the spinner is spun and try their luck with the next difference. When a player covers a row, column, or diagonal, she has bingo. All players then remove their markers, shuffle the cards, and start again.

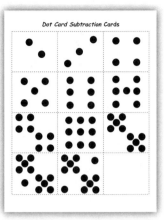

What's in the Bag?   *What's in the Bag?* is a simple subtraction activity in which students are given a paper bag containing 12 cubes or counters. One partner reaches into the bag and pulls out some counters. Partners count to find the total. The other partner spins a −1/−2 spinner (see CD), and then partners predict how many 1 less or 2 less will be. Students count to check their predictions, and write the number sentence. Then, the counters are returned to the bag and partners repeat the task.

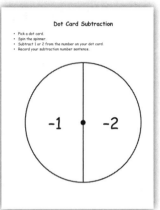

Dot Card Subtraction   In *Dot Card Subtraction* (see CD), students take turns picking a 2–12 dot card and then spinning a −1/−2 spinner to determine if they subtract 1 or subtract 2. Students record the subtraction number sentences.

Spinning More or Less   *Spinning More or Less* provides combined practice of addition and subtraction facts. In this game, students take turns finding 1 more, 2 more, 1 less, or 2 less than a number. Players shuffle a set of ten-frame cards (see CD) and put them in a deck facedown. Players then spread out their own sets of number cards (1–12), faceup, in front of them. Players take turns flipping over a ten-frame card and spinning the +1/+2/−1/−2 spinner to find out what to add or subtract from the ten-frame amount. If the sum or difference appears on one of the players' number cards, he flips the card over. If it

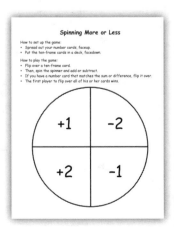

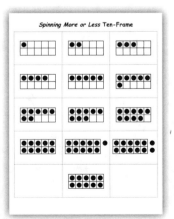

doesn't, he returns the ten-frame card to the bottom of the deck. The first player to flip over all of his number cards is the winner.

Monitoring Progress

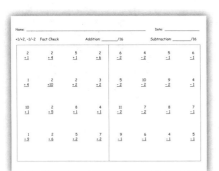

Mixed Fact Checks, which include subtraction facts, are included on the CD. Once students have had experiences with +1/+2 addition facts, have had opportunities to explore the concept of 1 less and 2 less, and have engaged in −1/−2 practice tasks, the Mixed Fact Checks allow us to monitor their progress toward fluency. Keep in mind that students need additional time to complete these Mixed Fact Checks which contain more facts and require students to shift their thinking from addition to subtraction.

CHAPTER THREE

Adding 0

+	0	1	2	3	4	5	6	7	8	9	10
0	0	1	2	3	4	5	6	7	8	9	10
1	1	2	3	4	5	6	7	8	9	10	11
2	2	3	4	5	6	7	8	9	10	11	12
3	3	4	5	6	7	8	9	10	11	12	13
4	4	5	6	7	8	9	10	11	12	13	14
5	5	6	7	8	9	10	11	12	13	14	15
6	6	7	8	9	10	11	12	13	14	15	16
7	7	8	9	10	11	12	13	14	15	16	17
8	8	9	10	11	12	13	14	15	16	17	18
9	9	10	11	12	13	14	15	16	17	18	19
10	10	11	12	13	14	15	16	17	18	19	20

KNOWN FACTS   **+0** TARGETED FACTS   UNKNOWN FACTS

We began our study of math facts by focusing on +1/+2 and −1/−2 facts. Beginning with these simple facts allowed our students to gently build on their previous understandings about numbers, including their understanding of the counting process and one-to-one correspondence. Our students have now had time to absorb the meanings of addition and subtraction, explore simple addition and subtraction math facts, and acquire a small set of known facts. They are now ready to enlarge that set of known facts as we introduce addition and subtraction with 0.

51

The 0 facts are certainly the simplest set of facts when it comes to automaticity. Adding or subtracting nothing does not change a quantity. However, while these facts are easy for automaticity, thinking about part of a quantity when the part consists of nothing is a bit confusing. And how are we separating or taking away if we remove nothing? Rather than beginning our study of addition and subtraction with these atypical facts, they are better addressed after our students have had some experiences with +1/+2 facts and have developed a firmer understanding of the addition and subtraction processes. Once that understanding is developed, 0 facts come easy for our students.

Focusing on the Big Ideas

Exploring big ideas about mathematics provides the backdrop for our exploration of addition and subtraction with 0. Some big ideas follow.

The zero property of addition tells us that 0 added to any number results in a sum that is the original quantity.

An understanding of 0, and the ways in which it impacts addition and subtraction equations, is important. Adding 0 to a quantity does not change the quantity. Subtracting 0 from a quantity does not change the quantity. Subtracting any number from itself results in 0. Armed with these understandings, 0 facts are quite simple to remember.

The order of the addends does not change the sum (the commutative property).

Whether we are finding the sum of $0 + 4$ or $4 + 0$, the sum will always be 0. The order of the addends does not matter.

Addition is a joining or part-part-whole process.

If one addend is 0, then nothing is being added or joined. If Kathy has 5 flowers in a vase and adds no more flowers to the vase, she still has 5 flowers ($5 + 0 = 5$). The joining process does not increase the quantity. In the same way, if one *part* is 0, then the other *part* must be equal to the *whole*. If Lisa has 6 cinnamon bagels and no chocolate chip bagels, she has 6 bagels altogether ($6 + 0 = 6$).

Subtraction is a separate or compare process.

If nothing is being separated from a set, the quantity in the set remains the same. If Dan has 7 pears and does not eat any, he still has 7 pears ($7 - 0 = 7$). If you compare the quantity in a set to 0, the difference will always be the quantity within the set. If Dan has 7 pears and Jerri has no pears, Dan has 7 more pears ($7 - 0 = 7$).

If you separate, or remove, the quantity of a whole set from the set, you will have nothing remaining. If Colleen has 3 ice cream cones and eats 3 of them, she has no cones left ($3 - 3 = 0$). If you compare 2 sets of 3 objects, they are the same, so the difference is 0. If Megan has 3 red bracelets and 3 blue bracelets, the difference is 0. She does not have any more or less of one than the other ($3 - 3 = 0$).

Key questions related to the big ideas for 0 facts are:

When you add 0, what happens to the sum? Why?

Does the order of the addends affect the sum? Give examples to justify your thinking.

If you know 5 + 0, will you know 0 + 5? Why?

What is 100 + 0? Explain how you know.

If you subtract 0 from a number, will it change the original number? Why or why not?

What is the answer when you subtract a number from itself? What is 5 − 5? What is 4 − 4? Does that make sense? Why?

Our goal is to continually reinforce the big ideas related to math facts as we help students develop addition and subtraction strategies.

Understanding +0 Facts

Literature Link: *Gray Rabbit's 1, 2, 3*

In Alan Baker's *Gray Rabbit's 1, 2, 3* (1994), a rabbit finds clay and creates a variety of animal friends before becoming weary and falling asleep. The story provides an opportunity to explore the sum of numbers when 0 is an addend.

Before Reading Show students the book's cover illustration. Tell them you will be reading a story about a rabbit that makes some friends out of clay. Ask students to think about the types of animal friends the rabbit might make. Have students turn and tell a partner a few of their ideas. Ask them to listen to the story to find out which animal friends, and how many of each, Gray Rabbit created.

During Reading As you read the story, pause slightly to have students predict each subsequent animal using the descriptive clues and the pictures of partially molded clay. Stop reading after you show the page with 10 mice.

Do not read the last two pages of the book, which show Gray Rabbit falling asleep, until later in the lesson.

After Reading   Discuss the animals that the rabbit made with clay. Begin a class chart to record the animals and the quantity of each kind of animal (e.g., 1 worm, 2 toucans, etc.). Have students record the totals on their *How Many Animals?* recording sheet (see CD).

Tell students that Gray Rabbit loved his animals so much he decided to make more, but there was a problem. Read the last two pages of the book, in which Gray Rabbit was so tired from making his animals that he fell sound asleep. He didn't make any more worms or toucans or bears or any other animals. He added 0 animals to each group! Using their *How Many Animals?* recording sheet, have students work in pairs to write number sentences to show the total amount of each type of animal, knowing that Gray Rabbit fell asleep and didn't make any more of the animals (see Figure 3.1). You might model for 1 worm (i.e., Gray Rabbit made 1 worm and then added 0 more worms, so he had $1 + 0 = 1$). After students have created number sentences for all of the animals on their sheet, have them share their findings to allow you to check for accuracy. Finally, ask students to look at the number sentences they created and to talk with partners about what they observe about the sum of any number and 0. Have some partners share their ideas with the class as you record their ideas on chart paper. Insights will likely include:

> *It didn't get any more.*
> *It was the same.*
> *He still had the same amount.*
> *0 isn't adding any.*
> *It's just the same number.*

Exploring the Facts: Acting Out +0 Facts

Capitalize on the benefits of movement and language by having students act out scenarios to represent math facts. When acting out +1 or +2 facts, students see the joining process as $5 + 1$ might be acted out with 5 girls jumping up and down and 1 girl joining them to jump up and down. How many girls were jumping up and down altogether? Students count as you record on the board: $5 + 1 = 6$. Pose questions to encourage talk about the addition facts like:

> *What does the 5 represent?*
> *What does the 1 represent?*

Why are we adding?

How did you find the answer?

Acting out problems is fun, engaging, and visual. Students truly see the math fact. But how do you help them see addition with 0?

Students can have fun acting out 0 facts, too.

> 7 students are waiting in line to get a drink of water. No more students join them. How many students are waiting in line?

Record $7 + 0 = 7$ on the board. Ask questions that get students talking about adding 0 and allow you to assess their understanding of the concept.

Figure 3.1 *This student creates number sentences to show what happens when 0 animals are added.*

How Many Animals?

Gray Rabbit made animal friends from clay.

Animals	How Many?	What if he added 0 more?
worm	1	$1 + 0 = 1$
toucans	2	$2 + 0 = 2$
bears	3	$3 + 0 = 3$
dogs	4	$4 + 0 = 4$
frogs	5	$5 + 0 = 5$
snakes	6	$6 + 0 = 6$
snails	7	$7 + 0 = 7$
elephants	8	$8 + 0 = 8$
bugs	9	$9 + 0 = 9$
mice	10	$10 + 0 = 10$

What does the 7 represent?

What does the 0 represent?

Why didn't anyone else get in line to get a drink?

What does it mean to add 0?

How did you find the answer?

Acting out math facts is quick and simple. You will find opportunities all around you. Focusing on boys and girls is a great way to explore part-part-whole addition scenarios like the following.

> 4 boys were at the math center. No girls were at the math center. How many students were at the math center?

> 9 boys had chocolate milk for lunch. No girls had chocolate milk for lunch. How many students had chocolate milk for lunch?

Modify the acting out process by replacing real people with manipulatives. Counters can represent the boys and girls, as students count out 9 counters for the boys who had chocolate milk and add no more counters, because no girls had chocolate milk. Have students record the number sentences along with you as you record them on the board.

Add a reflective component to the lesson by asking students to share insights they have noticed about +0 math facts. After acting out or using manipulatives for several scenarios, move students to a language-based task by using the *Adding Zero* activity on the CD. Students find the sums for +0 facts and then record their insights to the following prompts.

What do you notice about the sums?

Is it easy or hard to add 0? Explain.

Providing students with concrete experiences, accompanied by symbolic representations, and followed by opportunities to talk and write about their insights (see Figure 3.2) allows them to deepen their understanding of the concept.

Supporting All Learners

The following classroom activities provide you with additional lesson ideas for the whole class or for small teacher-led groups of students who might need to explore +0 facts in a different way.

Figure 3.2 *This student shares her insights about adding 0 after observing a series of +0 equations.*

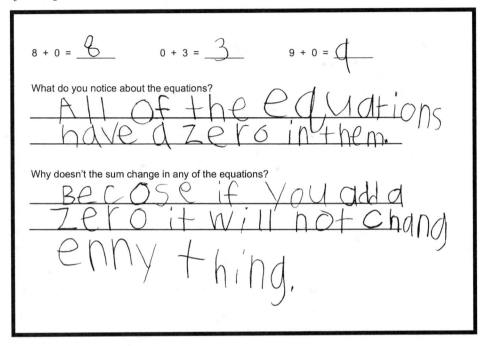

8 + 0 = 8   0 + 3 = 3   9 + 0 = 9

What do you notice about the equations?

All of the equations have a zero in them.

Why doesn't the sum change in any of the equations?

Becose if you add a zero it will not chang enny thing.

Using Part-Part-Whole Mats to Visualize +0 Facts   Once students grasp the idea that addition with 0 is simply adding nothing to a quantity, +0 facts become simple. By using a part-part-whole mat (see CD), and placing cubes or counters on sections of the mat, students can quickly visualize addition with 0. The two upper sections are where addends are represented (the *parts*) and the larger section at the bottom is where the sum is represented (the *whole* or *total*). When exploring 8 + 0, students place 8 cubes in one of the top sections, 0 cubes in the other top section, and then move all of the cubes to the bottom section to show the sum. Students will quickly see that the sum is always the same as the non-zero addend, because one *part* on their mat is always empty.

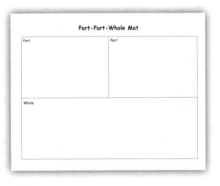

The part-part-whole mat can also be used as a place for students to illustrate addition facts. For 8 + 0, a student might draw 8 fish in the top left section, no fish in the top right section, and 8 fish in the bottom section to represent the sum. Having students record the number sentence in the bottom section will help them connect the concrete/pictorial to the abstract representation of the math fact.

Adding 0 to Ten-Frames   Identifying that +0 means adding nothing is a critical understanding. Have a set of ten-frame cards (see CD) and ask students to tell you the number of dots on the card and the number that would

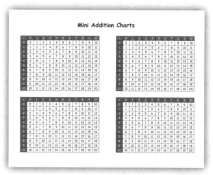

Tip While all students are involved in practice for fluency, pull up a seat by a small group of students who may be having more difficulty with the facts and provide some quick tips, or interview individual students to assess their mastery. See the CD for ideas on conducting automaticity interviews.

be there if they add 0. Have them tell or write the number sentence to go with the +0 fact.

Building Automaticity

Students generally master +0 facts quickly. Remind them that adding 0 is not changing the quantity at all. The sum will be the other addend, regardless of its position in the equation. This understanding makes automaticity with +0 facts a simple task.

Targeted Practice

Paired Practice Student-sized fact cards (see CD) are the perfect size for use in games, interactive activities, and partner fact reviews. Make five-minute paired practice sessions a classroom routine to provide quick opportunities for students to work in pairs to revisit the facts. Students might work together to find the sums or take on the roles of *teacher* and *student* with one partner posing the facts (teacher) and the other stating the sums (student). Provide partners with addition charts (see CD) so they are able to check the answers to any unknown facts. Remember to add some fact cards from previously taught math facts (e.g., +1/+2 and −1/−2 facts) to provide continued review.

Managing Math Games In order for math game time to go smoothly, students must know the rules for the game and they must know your expectations for their behavior as they play the game (see Figure 3.3). Consider the following questions.

- Where can they play the game? At their seat? On the floor? At a designated center?

- What is an acceptable voice level?

- How many times can they play the game? Is there a time limit? What if they finish the game before game time is over? What do they do next?

- Is winning an important component of the game?

- Should they hand in their recording sheets? If so, where?

- What is their responsibility for cleaning up after they finish the game?

- What is the consequence if they do not play appropriately?

It is not important that we all have the same answer for the questions above, but it is important that your students know your answers to each question.

There are many silent math fact practice tasks that can take the place of math games for a student who is ignoring your procedures. Taking away the privilege of game play for the day is a reasonable consequence. Each student can start fresh again tomorrow, hopefully remembering that ignoring your procedures will result in the natural consequence of practicing alone. See the CD for a reflection sheet that prompts students to reflect on their misbehavior and plan for more appropriate participation next time.

Who Has More?   In *Who Has More?* (see CD), students take turns selecting a 0 fact card from a facedown stack. Each student records his equation. The student with the greater sum circles his equation and wins that round. Then, players select another fact card and play again.

Domino Addition   Give partners a set of double-nine dominoes or domino templates (see CD). Have them find dominoes with 0 on one side and then write addition equations to show the sums (e.g., $3 + 0 = 3$). Strengthen students' understanding of the commutative property by asking them to turn the domino and write another addition equation (e.g., $0 + 3 = 3$).

Figure 3.3 *These students are able to play the game independently, freeing the teacher to work with a small group of students who might need additional support with the facts.*

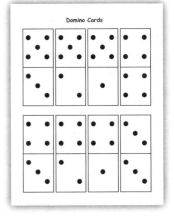

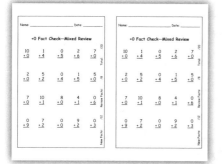

Monitoring Progress

Highlighting Success   Fact Checks allow us to monitor students' progress toward math fact fluency. Rather than asking students to compete against other students, which discourages students who struggle with memory tasks, consider having students set personal goals. Can they beat their own previous record by knowing more facts than on their previous Fact Check?

Following Fact Checks, have students use yellow highlighters to indicate known facts on a completed addition chart (see chart on CD). By highlighting known facts, students will also be able to quickly focus on facts that still need to be mastered. Encourage students to select a few facts as their goal for the next Fact Check.

Using Varied Versions of Fact Checks   Fact Checks can be used to measure student progress on a specific set of addition facts currently being studied, a set of addition and subtraction facts for the current fact set, or a set of cumulative facts including facts from any previously taught fact sets (see CD for a variety of Fact Checks). The cumulative Fact Checks that assess both current and previously learned facts are organized to allow teachers to easily score the current facts and previously learned facts separately. The columns on the ends and the center column measure the current facts, and the other two columns measure previously learned facts. Simply tallying correct responses in each column will give a quick view of progress.

Connecting to Subtraction

Once students develop an understanding of addition with 0, provide opportunities for students to explore related subtraction facts and take every opportunity to talk about the connection between addition and subtraction facts.

Exploring Subtraction Models: Revisiting *Gray Rabbit's 1, 2, 3*

Reread *Gray Rabbit's 1, 2, 3*. Remind students that Gray Rabbit made 6 "sliding, gliding snakes." Tell students that they will be working with partners to create their own clay snakes. Prepare some number cards 2–9, but be sure that there are 2 cards for each number (e.g., 2 twos, 2 threes, 2 fours, etc.). For small classes, you might just have cards for the numbers 4–9 or 5–9. Each pair will select a number card to find out how many snakes they should create with their clay. Once students have made their clay snakes, ask them to turn and tell their partners how many they would have if 0 snakes slithered away. Ask them to share how they would write a subtraction equation to show that. Create a chart on the board to show the equations for various numbers of snakes. Ask students to share their insights about subtracting 0. You will likely hear:

> *It doesn't change the number.*
> *It's the same.*
> *Nothing is taken away.*

Next, have pairs find the other set of partners that have the same number of snakes as they do (because you had 2 of each number card as you assigned quantities of snakes, 2 pairs should have made the same quantity of snakes). Have them compare their sets of snakes to see who has more. Have them share their answers (all teams should say they are the same—neither team made more). Ask students how they would write a number sentence to compare the 2 sets of snakes. What operation do they use when they compare? Providing an example might help: *If one pair had 6 snakes and one had 4, how many more would the first pair have?* Did they use subtraction? Would that work for our snake problem? What would the number sentence look like? If both pairs had 6 snakes, would $6 - 6 = 0$ make sense? What does the 0 represent? Have them write and share number sentences for their comparisons of snakes.

Activities to Promote Fluency

Domino Subtraction Give partners a set of dominoes or domino templates (see CD). Have them find dominoes with 0 on one side and write subtraction equations to show the difference ($5 - 0 = 5$). Or ask them to find dominoes with the same number on each side and write subtraction number sentences to show the difference ($5 - 5 = 0$).

Fact Family Homes Give partners a set of 1–10 number cards. Have students shuffle the cards and place them in a pile facedown. Have students select a card and write that number and 0 on the door of their fact family house (see CD). Have them write one of the four fact family number sentences in each of the windows of the house as in Figure 3.4.

Tip **Recipe for Homemade Modeling Dough**

1 c. flour
$\frac{1}{2}$ c. salt
2 tsp. cream of tartar
1 c. water
2 tbsp. oil
1 tsp. food coloring (any color)

Combine all dry ingredients in a saucepan. Gradually stir in 1 cup of water mixed with oil, and add food coloring. Cook over medium to high heat, stirring constantly until a ball forms. Remove from heat, place dough on the table, and knead until smooth. Store the dough in a plastic bag.

Figure 3.4 *Practice with fact families reinforces the connection between addition and subtraction.*

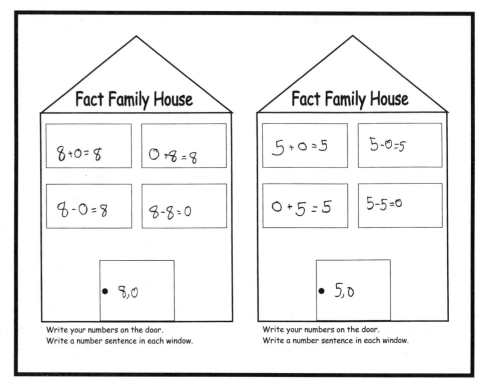

CHAPTER FOUR

Adding 10

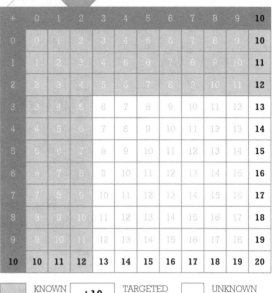

+	0	1	2	3	4	5	6	7	8	9	10
0	0	1	2	3	4	5	6	7	8	9	10
1	1	2	3	4	5	6	7	8	9	10	11
2	2	3	4	5	6	7	8	9	10	11	12
3	3	4	5	6	7	8	9	10	11	12	13
4	4	5	6	7	8	9	10	11	12	13	14
5	5	6	7	8	9	10	11	12	13	14	15
6	6	7	8	9	10	11	12	13	14	15	16
7	7	8	9	10	11	12	13	14	15	16	17
8	8	9	10	11	12	13	14	15	16	17	18
9	9	10	11	12	13	14	15	16	17	18	19
10	10	11	12	13	14	15	16	17	18	19	20

KNOWN FACTS   +10 TARGETED FACTS   UNKNOWN FACTS

By focusing on math facts with simple addends of 0, 1, and 2, our students now know fifty-seven math facts! We recognize that these are simpler facts and that many of the still unknown facts are more complex, but our students are building a repertoire of known facts, extending their understanding of numbers, and gaining a sense of accomplishment. Our next focus is on facts that will help us build a strong foundation for many of the unknown facts to come—facts with 10 as an addend.

Automatic recall of facts with 10 as an addend gives our students the ability to use +10 facts to simplify finding the sum of other, more complex, unknown facts. Focusing on +10 thinking is an investment in efficiency for future strategies like making ten and using tens. In addition, it expands students' number sense and extends their understanding of number concepts as they explore this very significant number within our number system.

Focusing on the Big Ideas

Exploring big ideas about mathematics provides the backdrop for our exploration of addition with 10 as an addend. Some big ideas follow.

Numbers can represent separate objects or groups of 10 objects.

Objects can be counted separately or grouped in tens. The concept of place value allows us to know what each number represents. Our students begin to understand what a two-digit number represents as we begin with 5 objects, then add 10 more to get 15 total objects.

Adding 10 to a single-digit number will add one place value.

Adding 10 to any single-digit number will result in a two-digit number with a 1 in the tens place. This makes sense because we are adding *1 ten*.

The order of the addends does not change the sum (the commutative property).

Whether we are focusing on 5 + 10 or 10 + 5, the sum will be the same. The order of the addends does not change the sum.

Key questions related to the big ideas for +10 addition are:

When you add 10 to a one-digit number, how does it change the number?

Why is the sum a two-digit number?

How could you quickly find the sum of a number plus 10?

Does the order of the addends affect the sum? Give examples to justify your thinking.

What happens when you subtract 10 from a number? (Focus on numbers between 11 and 19.)

Our goal is to continually reinforce the big ideas related to math facts as we help students develop addition and subtraction strategies.

Understanding +10 Facts

Literature Link: *If You Give a Mouse a Cookie*

If You Give a Mouse a Cookie, by Laura Numeroff (1985), is a humorous story about what can happen if you give a visitor a snack. In this case, the visitor, a mouse, asks for more and more.

Before Reading   Tell students that you will be reading a story about cookies. Ask them if they prefer to eat chocolate chip, sugar, or oatmeal cookies. Use tally marks on the board to show their results or create a quick picture graph by having students tape a circle to represent a cookie to the appropriately labeled row on the class graph. Discuss the results. Can they tell you the number of students who picked each type of cookie? Can they tell you which type of cookie most students chose or the fewest chose? Can they compare two types of cookies to tell you how many more people liked one type than another? Tell students that you will be reading a story about a mouse who likes cookies. Show them the cover illustration and ask them what kind of cookie the mouse likes best—he is holding a chocolate chip cookie! Ask them to listen to see what happens after the mouse is given a cookie.

During Reading   When reading the story to students for the first time, move through the story without too many interruptions for discussion. Students are anxious to hear what will happen next and lengthy discussions in the midst of the story can be distracting and result in students forgetting the last event that occurred in the story, or simply losing interest in the story.

After Reading   Have students identify the sequence of events in the story. The mouse gets a cookie, then needs some milk, then needs a straw, then needs a napkin. He has to look in the mirror to see if he has a milk moustache, then needs some scissors to trim a hair, a broom to clean the hair on the floor, a place to take a nap, and someone to read him a bedtime story. He asks for more and more, and everything started by giving him one delicious chocolate chip cookie.

Ask students what makes a chocolate chip cookie so irresistible. Ask them if all chocolate chip cookies are the same. How might they differ? Although all chocolate chip cookies have chocolate chips, they might differ with some

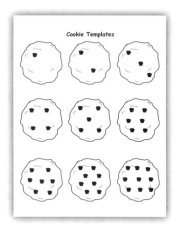

Cookie Templates

having more chips than others. Tell students that they will be exploring chocolate chip cookies and that theirs will not all be the same. Have students randomly select a cookie card (see templates on CD) to see how many chocolate chips are in their cookie. Have them draw a picture of their cookie, with exactly that number of chocolate chips, on the *Ten More Chocolate Chips* recording sheet (see CD).

Explain to students that we want their cookies to be super delicious, so we will be adding 10 more chocolate chips to each of their cookies. Ask students to find out how many chips their cookie will have after they add 10 more chips. They may draw the additional chips on their cookie drawing or find their answer in another way. Providing counters to represent chocolate chips supports those students who need to explore the problem in a concrete way. Ask them to record an addition number sentence to represent adding 10 chips to their cookies as in Figure 4.1. Have students select another cookie card, draw the cookie on their sheet, and then add 10 more chips. Do this several more times as you move through the room monitoring their work, asking questions to check for understanding, or guiding students who are struggling with the task.

Once students have gathered some data, begin a class discussion. Have students share the changes in the number of chocolate chips in their cookies as you record some of their number sentences on the board or chart paper (see Figure 4.2).

Ask students to turn to a partner and talk about any patterns they notice in the number sentences. Observations will likely include:

It is just counting 10 more.

You just add a 1 to the number of chips.

You just write 1 and then the number we already had.

Record a few ideas on the board or chart paper. Check to see that students have internalized the idea with a few quick questions.

How many chips would there be if I had 4 chips and added 10? Why?

How many chips would there be if I had 9 chips and added 10? Why?

How many chips would there be if I had 6 chips and added 10? Why?

Exploring the Facts: Using Double Ten-Frames

Ten-frames are a helpful visual tool. Numbers are represented based on the quantity of dots on the frame (e.g., six dots represent the number 6). The arrangement of dots in 2 rows of 5 allows students to quickly identify numbers.

Tip Rather than randomly selecting a cookie card to determine the original number of chocolate chips, students might spin a 1–9 spinner, roll a number cube, or even count the actual number of chocolate chips they see in a miniature chocolate chip cookie to find their starting number. Once students have the original number of chocolate chips, they calculate adding 10 more to their cookie.

Figure 4.1 *This student records number sentences to go with her chocolate chip investigations.*

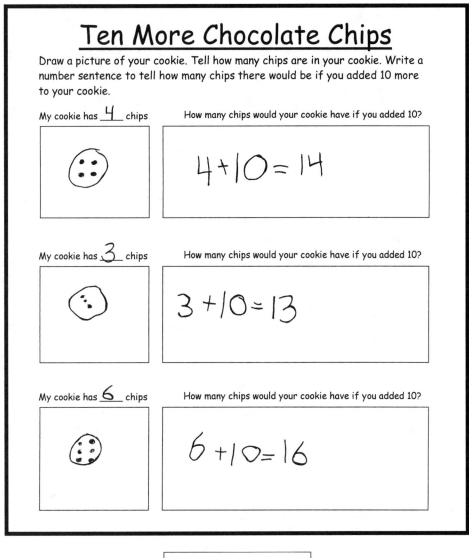

Ten More Chocolate Chips

Draw a picture of your cookie. Tell how many chips are in your cookie. Write a number sentence to tell how many chips there would be if you added 10 more to your cookie.

My cookie has __4__ chips

How many chips would your cookie have if you added 10?

$$4 + 10 = 14$$

My cookie has __3__ chips

How many chips would your cookie have if you added 10?

$$3 + 10 = 13$$

My cookie has __6__ chips

How many chips would your cookie have if you added 10?

$$6 + 10 = 16$$

1 + 10 = 11
2 + 10 = 12
3 + 10 = 13
4 + 10 = 14
5 + 10 = 15
6 + 10 = 16
7 + 10 = 17
8 + 10 = 18
9 + 10 = 19

Figure 4.2 *As students observe the class data, they gain insights about adding 10.*

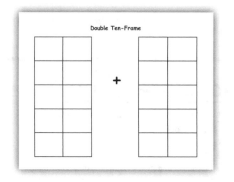

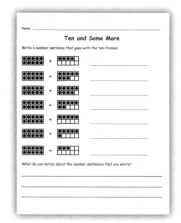

Because of their experiences with counting and number charts, students may initially find this fact set easier when 10 is the first addend (e.g., 10 + 4 = 14), particularly if they are finding sums by counting on from 10. The counting on strategy is most efficient when students begin with the larger number and add a small quantity, which is why our focus on counting on was limited to addends of 1 and 2. Although counting on certainly makes sense to students, our goal is to lead them to the discovery of insights about patterns and place value, replacing the cumbersome method of counting on with the quicker method of adding 1 ten (adding the digit *1* in the tens place to represent 10 more).

When every section of the ten-frame is filled, students immediately know that it represents 10. Pairs of ten-frames, one completely filled to represent 10, are an ideal way to explore +10 facts.

Use the addition ten-frames on the CD to model adding 10. Place 10 dots, or counters, on one side of the ten-frame and record *10* below it. Next to it, place 1 dot or counter on the ten-frame and record *1* below it. Place an addition sign between the numbers (e.g., 10 + 1) and ask students to turn and tell a partner the total number of dots, the sum for the two frames. Record the sum (i.e., *10 + 1 = 11*). Ask students to tell you how they arrived at the answer. Did they count all of the dots? Did they count on? Did they already know the +1 fact? Repeat the process with frames with 10 dots and 2 dots, recording *10 + 2 = 12*.

Provide partners with the *Ten and Some More* recording sheet (see CD). Have partners work together to find the sums when beginning with 10 and adding *3–9* more. When students have found the sums, have them work together to write some things they notice about the number sentences. Have them share some ideas with the class.

Supporting All Learners

The following classroom activities provide you with additional lesson ideas for the whole class or for small teacher-led groups of students who might need to explore +10 facts in a different way.

Exploring +10 on Number Charts   Provide students with 1–20 charts (see CD) and two transparent counters. Show them a +10 fact card in the "_____ + 10" format. Have students place their first counter on the first addend, then add 10 and place their second counter on the sum as in Figure 4.3. For a more guided approach, find the sum together and have students simply place their counter on that sum. Have them record the number sentence.

Twenty Chart

| 1 | 2 | 3 | 4 | 5 | 6 | 7 | 8 | 9 | 10 |
| 11 | 12 | 13 | 14 | 15 | 16 | 17 | 18 | 19 | 20 |

Twenty Chart

| 1 | 2 | 3 | 4 | 5 | 6 | 7 | 8 | 9 | 10 |
| 11 | 12 | 13 | 14 | 15 | 16 | 17 | 18 | 19 | 20 |

Twenty Chart

| 1 | 2 | 3 | 4 | 5 | 6 | 7 | 8 | 9 | 10 |
| 11 | 12 | 13 | 14 | 15 | 16 | 17 | 18 | 19 | 20 |

1	2	3	4	5	6	7	8	9	10
11	12	13	14	15	16	17	18	19	20

Figure 4.3 *Number charts enable students to see patterns.*

Try it again with a different fact card, placing both counters on the 1–20 chart and writing the number sentences. After several facts have been done, ask students what they notice about the sums (the sum is directly below the addend on the 1–20 chart). Can they explain why this is happening (see Figure 4.4)? Can students predict the next sum? Show another fact card and ask for students' prediction. Are they beginning to see a pattern? Try a few more with students first predicting and then showing the sum on their charts.

In a Flash *In a Flash* is a fun classroom activity that promotes quick recognition of facts. Students are given a quick glimpse of a fact, modeled on a double ten-frame, and asked to tell the sum. The model might be created using counters on the ten-frame and shown quickly by flashing the image on an overhead projector or SMART Board, or might be created by drawing ten-frames on chart paper and covering the drawings with another piece of paper to allow you to quickly uncover and cover again. The image is shown for just a second or two and then students are asked to tell the sum and discuss how they know (e.g., "One was filled, so it is 10, and the other just had 2, so it's 12."). If available, individual whiteboards might be used for students to record the number sentence they think they saw. After students share their sums and rationale, the image is shown again to check their answers. *In a Flash* can be modified to use with any set of facts and is a student favorite, so might be used as a treat at the end of class. Consider rewarding a couple of students by making them Flash Masters for the day.

Tip When placing counters on number charts, transparent counters allow students to see the number through the counter. If they are not available, try small paper clips as counters, or other items that will not block the number from students' sight.

Figure 4.4 *Observing the 1–20 chart allows this student to discover patterns when adding 10 4 becomes 14.*

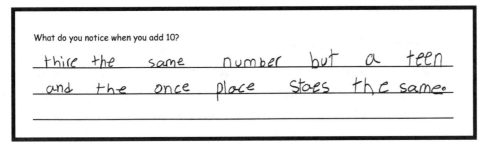

What do you notice when you add 10?

thire the same number but a teen and the once place staes the same.

Figure 4.5 *Find simple ways to engage students in math fact practice.*

Finger Facts   The fingers on our hands are one of the simplest real-world connections to 10. Have some hands-on fun with adding 10 by having students find the number of fingers on pairs of students. Invite one student to be the 10 finger student, showing all of his fingers to the group. Invite another student to join him, with that student showing any number of fingers she chooses as in Figure 4.5. Challenge others in the group to tell the total number of fingers. Talk about how they knew the sum. If the second student held up 9 fingers, did they recognize it as 9 immediately by knowing it was 1 less than 10? How did they know the sum of 10 and 9? After you do some with the group, have students try some in pairs, alternating which partner is the designated 10 finger student. Listen to students' thinking as they talk together about the sum of their fingers.

Building Automaticity

Targeted Practice

Our goal is for students to quickly retrieve sums from memory rather than using the process of counting, so ongoing practice is needed to allow students to automatically recall +10 facts. Games and interactive tasks keep students engaged in practice activities.

Focused Fact Practice   After introducing a new set of facts (e.g., +10 facts), select just those fact cards for the first rounds of practice. After several rounds of targeted practice with the new facts, incorporate previously learned facts (e.g., +1/+2, +0) to provide a balanced review.

Linking Cubes Addition   Each pair of students will need 20 linking cubes, a 1–10 spinner, and the *Linking Cubes Addition* recording sheet (see CD). Partners begin by making 1 chain by linking 10 cubes. One partner then spins the spinner and takes that number of cubes from the remaining single cubes. Partners work together to find the sum of 10 (their chain) and the number they spun (the single cubes). Students draw a picture to show what they have done and write the number sentence.

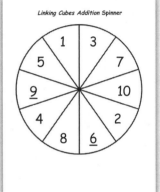

Ten More   In *Ten More*, students add 10 to see who has the larger sum. Provide each pair with a set of 0–10 dot cards (see CD). Have students find the dot card that represents 10 and place it faceup to use as a visual to support their computation during the game. Have students shuffle the other dot cards and place them facedown. Students take turns picking a card, adding 10, and recording the number sentence on their *Ten More* recording sheet (see CD). Players compare their sums and the player with the larger sum circles his number sentence and wins the round. Then, players return their dot cards to the pile, shuffle the cards, and play again. Having a 1–20 chart nearby, or displayed in the classroom, will allow students to check their accuracy in finding the larger sum.

Tools to Support Accuracy   We want our students to practice their skills in a meaningful and accurate way. After all, practicing inaccurate facts or inefficient methods does not promote fluency and leads to student frustration. Support students as they play math fact games by providing them with access to tools that support their accuracy. Number lines, 1–20 charts, addition charts, or even calculators are all possible tools. The CD has many accuracy tools that can be quickly copied and distributed to students who might need the support. Having opponents check a player's computation doubles the math fact practice. Games can be modified so that inaccurate calculations result in losing a turn or removing a game piece from the board. Providing accuracy tools places the emphasis on mastery of the facts.

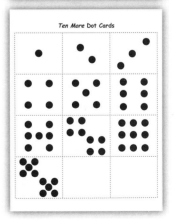

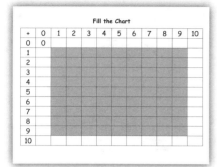

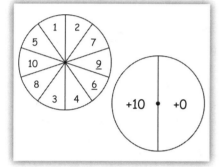

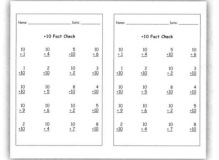

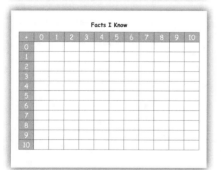

Fill the Chart Reviewing past facts will help move students toward fact fluency. *Fill the Chart* (see CD) addresses +10 facts and provides a review of +0 facts. Players take turns spinning a number and then spinning the +0/+10 spinner to see what should be added to their number. This game also provides practice using the addition chart, as students write the sum in the correct spot on the chart, which is shaded so only +0/+10 locations are open. The first player to fill her chart is the winner. If you prefer not to have a winner, simply have pairs work together to fill the chart.

Monitoring Progress

Adjustments to Fact Checks The Fact Checks look a bit different beginning with the +10 facts. Students now have experience with Fact Checks and are getting comfortable with the format. Rather than only sixteen facts, the number of facts on each Fact Check (see CD) has increased to twenty. This increase allows us to include all of the targeted facts, so we are better able to pinpoint specific facts that are troublesome for students.

If there are students who have difficulty with the new Fact Checks because of the number of facts that appear on the page, the CD allows you to customize the Fact Check by deleting some facts to create smaller sets of facts. It is important, however, that if some facts are deleted, you create two versions of the Fact Check, so that students will encounter every fact within a fact set. By alternating versions, students get experience with, and you will be able to assess their knowledge of, all of the facts in the set.

Tracking Progress Finding ways for students to keep track of their progress as they master addition facts will give them a sense of accomplishment and will focus them on next steps. Provide students with a blank addition chart. After practicing +1, +2, +0 and +10 facts, have students record their known facts on their *Facts I Know* chart (see CD). Remind students of the commutative property to help them recognize their many known facts (see Figure 4.6). Collect their charts or have them keep them in a safe place (i.e., glued inside the cover of a math journal). Each time a new fact set is mastered, have students fill the facts in on their addition chart. They will quickly see how many math facts they have mastered.

Connecting to Subtraction

Once students develop an understanding of adding 10, take every opportunity to talk about the connection between addition and subtraction facts.

Facts I Know

+	0	1	2	3	4	5	6	7	8	9	10
0	0	1	2	3	4	5	6	7	8	9	10
1	1	2	3	4	5	6	7	8	9	10	11
2	2	3	4	5	6	7	8	9	10	11	12
3	3	4	5								13
4	4	5	6								14
5	5	6	7								15
6	6	7	8								16
7	7	8	9								17
8	8	9	10								18
9	9	10	11								19
10	10	11	12	13	14	15	16	17	18	19	20

Figure 4.6 *Students recognize their accomplishments as they create a Facts I Know chart.*

Literature Link: *Don't Eat the Teacher!*

In *Don't Eat the Teacher!* by Nick Ward (1998), a shark learns a valuable lesson during his first day of school. Don't eat the teacher! Students will have fun with this story as they explore subtracting 10.

Before Reading   Ask students what types of creatures they would find in the ocean. Tell them you will be reading a silly story about a sea creature, a shark, that eats some unusual things. Ask them to listen for the unusual things this shark eats.

During Reading   While reading the book, share the pictures of Sammy, the shark, and the other sea creatures in his class. When you have finished reading the story, return to some pages and ask students to estimate the numbers of sea creatures on the page. Is it more than 10? Less than 10? How did they make their estimates? Count the creatures to see if their estimates were close.

After Reading   Ask students if they would be worried to be a fish in Sammy's class. Give each pair of students a problem card (see CD). Ask students to work together to read their problem, talk about how to solve it, and solve it

together. They should either draw a picture or use manipulatives, like counters or goldfish crackers, to show how they got their answers.

When a pair has solved a problem, ask the students to raise their hands so you can take a look at their work, ask questions to check their thinking, and then give them a different problem card. After students have had time to solve several problems, have students form a circle and share one of their problems, including their drawing, with the rest of the class. Record the different subtraction number sentences on the board or chart paper as students share. Have students talk about things they notice in the equations. You will likely hear:

> *When you subtract 10, it's just the other number.* (two-digit to one-digit)
>
> *The 1 goes away when you subtract 10.* (place value understanding—subtract 1 ten)
>
> *If you change it around and add it, you use the same numbers.* (fact families)

Record some of their insights on chart paper to summarize their important thinking.

Practicing for Fluency

Triangle Fact Cards   Triangle fact cards (see CD) provide a great opportunity to reinforce the connection between addition and subtraction facts and to work toward mastery of both. The three corners of the triangle hold the two addends and the sum. The sum is circled. As the teacher (or a partner) covers one corner, the student must either name the sum (if both addends are visible) or the missing addend (if an addend and sum are visible). Triangle fact cards can be used for partner practice, home practice, or for a small-group review led by the teacher. Additional triangle fact card activities include the following.

- Provide students with blank triangles and have them create their own set of triangle fact cards.

- Provide students with fact cards. As they select a card, they must write the four addition/subtraction number sentences represented by the card (fact families) as in Figure 4.7.

Linking Cubes Subtraction   For *Linking Cubes Subtraction*, students will need an 11–19 spinner, 19 linking cubes, and a *Linking Cubes* recording sheet (see CD). Students spin the spinner and take that quantity of linking cubes.

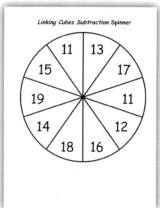

Figure 4.7 *Selecting a triangle fact card, and writing the four equations it represents, provides practice with both addition and subtraction facts.*

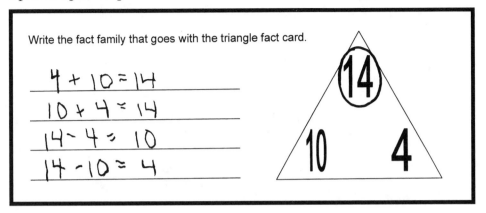

Students then subtract 10 and find the difference. Students might link 10 in a chain to see how many cubes are unattached to their chain, or they might draw a picture to find the difference. Students should record the subtraction equation and draw a diagram to show each subtraction fact as they repeatedly spin and subtract 10.

Scratch 'Em Off *Scratch 'Em Off* (see CD) is an elimination game in which students spin a spinner and subtract, find the difference in one of the boxes below their spinner, and cross it off. Students may only cross off one number per spin. If the difference has already been crossed off, the player loses his turn. The first player to cross off all of his numbers wins. To reuse game boards, have students cover the differences with beans or counters.

Three in a Row To play *Three in a Row* (see CD), players shuffle 10 fact cards and place them facedown in a deck. Players take turns pulling a card, subtracting to find the difference, and then putting a marker on the difference. The first player to cover three in a row is the winner.

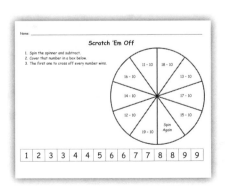

Tip **Reusing Game Boards**

Many math fact games require students to write on a game board to keep track of their progress. To avoid wasting paper, game boards can be copied and placed in plastic sleeves. Students then write on the plastic sleeves with dry erase markers. After the game, the sleeves can be cleaned and the game reused. Students can be responsible for cleaning their own game boards or the task might become an assigned classroom job.

CHAPTER FIVE

Doubles

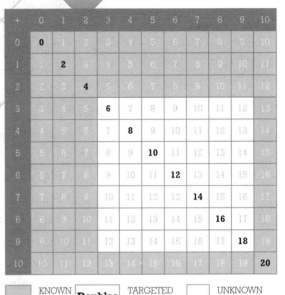

+	0	1	2	3	4	5	6	7	8	9	10
0	**0**	1	2	3	4	5	6	7	8	9	10
1	1	**2**	3	4	5	6	7	8	9	10	11
2	2	3	**4**	5	6	7	8	9	10	11	12
3	3	4	5	**6**	7	8	9	10	11	12	13
4	4	5	6	7	**8**	9	10	11	12	13	14
5	5	6	7	8	9	**10**	11	12	13	14	15
6	6	7	8	9	10	11	**12**	13	14	15	16
7	7	8	9	10	11	12	13	**14**	15	16	17
8	8	9	10	11	12	13	14	15	**16**	17	18
9	9	10	11	12	13	14	15	16	17	**18**	19
10	10	11	12	13	14	15	16	17	18	19	**20**

KNOWN FACTS   **Doubles**   TARGETED FACTS   UNKNOWN FACTS

We continue to add to our students' repertoire of math facts, this time focusing on doubles facts. Because both addends are the same, there is no need to address the commutative property, so this fact set is quite small—just eleven doubles facts in all. And because students have already explored and practiced +0, +1, +2, and +10 facts, they already know the sums for 0 + 0, 1 + 1, 2 + 2, and 10 + 10, leaving only seven unknown doubles facts. These facts are usually easy for students to recall and provide important links to future facts. Students will later refer back to these facts to find the sums of more complex near-doubles facts.

Focusing on the Big Ideas

Exploring big ideas about mathematics provides the backdrop for our exploration of doubles facts. Some big ideas include the following.

Doubling is the process of joining two groups of the same quantity.

The term *doubling* refers to the process of adding a quantity to itself. Doubling is joining two *like* groups. It is when both parts that make up a whole are equal quantities.

Halving is the opposite of doubling.

Separating a set into two equal groups results in halves. By halving a set, we can determine the quantity for the two equal parts that make the whole. Separating half from a set will result in a difference that is the same as the amount that was separated (i.e., in $12 - 6 = 6$, 6 was separated from the set and 6 remain in the set).

Addition and subtraction are inverse operations.

If students know that doubling 5 results in 10, or $5 + 5 = 10$, then they will also know that halving 10 results in 5, or $10 - 5 = 5$. Knowing a doubles fact (addition) supports students in knowing halves (subtraction).

Key questions related to the big ideas for doubles are:

What does it mean to double an amount?

What does it mean to find half of an amount?

How are doubling and halving alike? How are they different?

Our goal is to continually reinforce the big ideas related to math facts as we help students develop addition and subtraction strategies.

Understanding Doubles

Literature Link: *Double the Ducks*

In *Double the Ducks* (2003), Stuart J. Murphy tells the story of a boy with 5 ducks. When 5 duck friends follow them home, the boy must double everything as he cares for the 10 ducks.

Before Reading   Ask students to brainstorm types of animals that live on a farm. Ask them what kinds of things a farmer does to take care of the different animals. Ask students what it means to double something. Can they give an example of a double? Read the title and ask students to predict what the story might be about.

During Reading   As you read each number in the story and what it represents, record the number and item on chart paper (e.g., 1 person, 2 hands, 3 sacks of food, etc.). Pause after reading that each duck brought back a friend. Ask students to predict what the farmer will need in order to take care of 10 ducks. Continue reading to check their predictions.

After Reading   After finishing the story, compare the predictions that students made with the actual events of the story. Talk about what it means to double by referring to the items on the chart paper as examples. Pose a few related farm problems, having students turn and share the double with a partner. Keep the quantities small to assess students' understanding of the concept of doubling rather than their computation skills.

> His ducks love to eat bread. He needs 4 loaves of bread to feed his ducks. How many loaves of bread will he need if we double the ducks? How do you know?

> His pigs are very muddy. He uses 3 bars of soap to bathe them. How many bars of soap will he use if we double the pigs? How do you know?

> His horses love to eat sugar cubes. He needs 5 bags of sugar cubes for his horses. How many bags of sugar cubes will he need if we double the horses? How do you know?

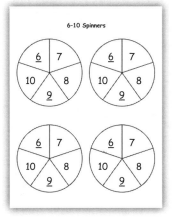

Once you are confident that students understand the concept of doubling, begin a task to explore doubles with addends of 6–10. Give students a *Double the Animals* recording sheet (see CD) and a set of 20 counters to represent animals. Students will work with partners to find the doubles sum for a set of cows, pigs, goats, and horses. Have partners work together, with one partner spinning a 6–10 spinner (see CD) to see how many cows are on the farm, and the other partner placing counters in a row to represent that number of cows. Partners then double the cows by creating a similar row to show the doubles set. Partners find the total number of cows, the sum, and record the addition number sentence on their recording sheets. Have partners switch roles and spin again, finding the number of pigs and the double for that number of pigs. As they work together to double all of the animals, observe how they are finding the sums. Do they know what it means to double? Are they counting all of the counters? Are they using any strategies? Do they have automatic recall of any doubles facts? Make a note of students who already have recall of some doubles facts. For the next lesson, those students might be transitioned to some of the doubles practice tasks, and those who were noted to be struggling with the concept might be asked to join you for additional explorations and discussions of the doubling process.

Once pairs have determined doubles for their animals, have them share some of their doubles facts, recording the number sentences on the board to provide a check for accuracy of the 6–10 doubles facts.

Finally, have students respond to the following prompt, as in Figure 5.1, in their math journals.

> **What does it mean to double a number?**

If students have a difficult time explaining their understanding of doubles in words, remind them that they can draw pictures or give examples to show

Figure 5.1 *This student shares her understanding of doubling.*

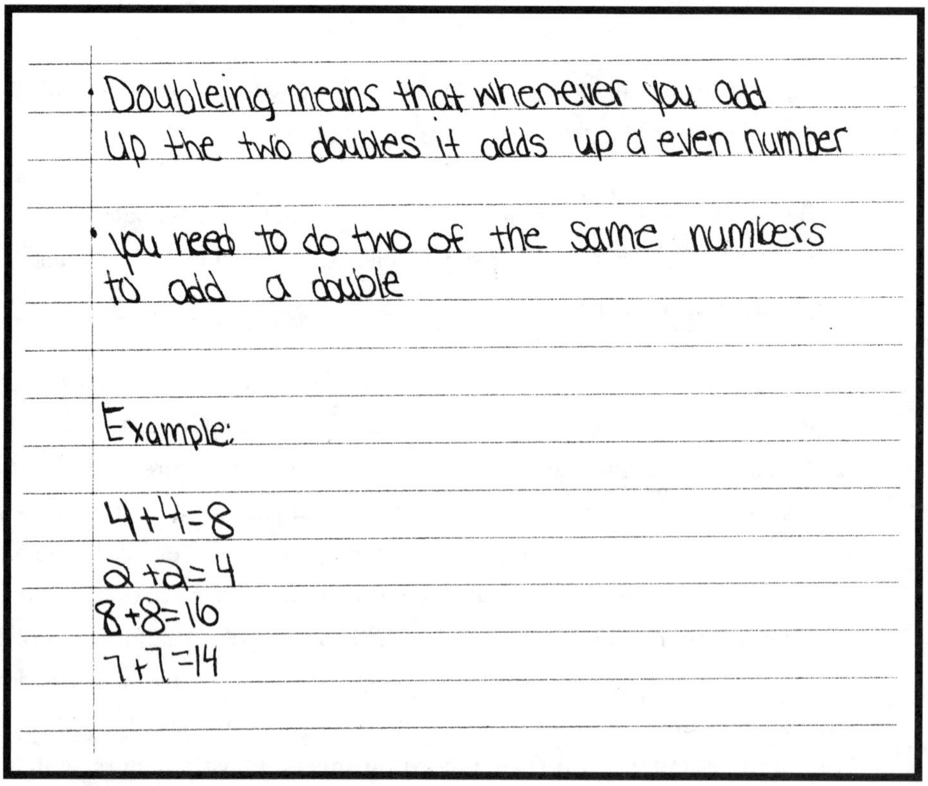

> • Doubleing means that whenever you add up the two doubles it adds up a even number
>
> • you need to do two of the same numbers to add a double
>
> Example:
>
> 4+4=8
> 2+2=4
> 8+8=16
> 7+7=14

their thinking. Sharing their writing with a partner, or presenting it during circle time, is an effective way to summarize the doubling concept.

Exploring the Facts: Creating Equal Sets

Visualizing the doubling process helps students better understand its connection to an addition equation. When considering the part-part-whole concept, both parts are of equal size. Model equal sets for students by creating sets on an overhead projector, document camera, or SMART Board. Lining objects in two equal rows helps students quickly see that sets are equal.

Pose some doubles problems.

> 4 orange fish were in the fish bowl. 4 black fish were in the fish bowl. How many fish were in the fish bowl?

> 6 boys were at the park. 6 girls were at the park. How many children were at the park?

> Bailey had 7 flower stickers. She had 7 bunny stickers. How many stickers did she have?

> Liam had 6 red cars and 6 blue cars. How many cars did he have?

> Colin had 9 soccer balls. He had 9 baseballs. How many balls did he have?

Allow students to use manipulatives to create the two equal-sized groups. A part-part-whole mat (see CD) provides a great template for this exploration. Students place a group of manipulatives in the top left section, then create an equal-sized group in the top right section. Pause to ask students about the two groups. Are they the same size? Have them record an addition equation to show the two parts, and then pull the two parts together to make one whole group. Have them find and record the sum. Continue to pose problems as you observe students at work.

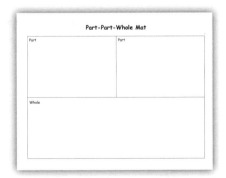

Tip The use of motion, pulling groups together, provides an important visualization of the concept of joining, or finding a total or whole set. An overhead projector or document camera allows us to physically move sets together, as do many SMART Boards. Magnetic graphics or student actors can also be joined to demonstrate the action of addition.

Supporting All Learners

The following classroom activities provide you with additional lesson ideas for the whole class or for small teacher-led groups with students who might need to explore doubles in a different way.

Act Out Doubles   Pose doubles problems for students to act out. You might have 4 students put their hands on their heads and then double the number of students putting their hands on their heads. You might have 6 students jump up and down and then double the number jumping up and down. Have fun doubling the students and recording the addition number sentences to represent the doubles.

Roll and Double It   Provide students with 20 counters. Roll a 1–6 number cube and ask students to make a row with that number of counters. Ask them to double it by making another row of the same size. Have them count to find the sum. Record the addition number sentence. Roll another number and repeat the process.

Ask students how they will know they are doubling when they see an addition number sentence. Do they notice that both addends in the number sentence are the same? Do they understand that means the size of each group is the same? Ask questions to guide students in observing the connection between the numbers in the equation (the same numbers) and the number of counters in each group (the same size groups).

Revisit *Double the Ducks*   For struggling students, it may be helpful to reread *Double the Ducks* and allow them to use manipulatives to double each item in the story. Students can use the *Doubles for Ducks* recording sheet (see CD) to show their work. Watch them as they work, asking questions to guide their thinking and assess their understanding. After completing the story items, brainstorm other farm items and have them select a few and find the doubles.

Magical Doubles   Share this doubles story to engage students in solving and writing doubles problems.

> Mork was a famous magician. Children loved to see his magic shows. Mork made a penny disappear and then reappear behind someone's ear. Amazing! He cut a scarf in half and with a wave of his wand made it a whole scarf again. Unbelievable! But most of all, children loved when Mork took out his magic hat. Mork put 1 cuddly bunny into his hat, waved his wand and chanted: "Magic hat, don't give me trouble. These children want to see a double!" He reached into the hat and pulled out 2 cuddly bunnies! The children cheered and shouted for more. Mork reached into his pocket and pulled out 2 shiny quarters, put them into his hat, waved his magic wand, and chanted: "Magic hat, don't give me trouble. These children want to see a double!" He reached into his hat and pulled out 4 shiny quarters!

Ask students to turn and tell a partner what Mork pulled out of his magic hat when he put these items into it:

3 purple purses

4 red balls

5 salty pretzels

6 juicy grapes

7 silver spoons

8 spotted owls

9 rotten potatoes

10 gray mice

Allow students to use beans or counters to explore the sums, if needed. Record each doubles number sentence on the board.

Have students talk with partners to decide on something else to put in Mork's hat. Go around the room to have pairs tell you what Mork put in and what he took out.

Class Doubles Book   As a class, make a list of things that come in 1, 2, 3, 4, and so on (i.e., 1 trunk on an elephant, 2 horns on a bull, 3 lights on a traffic light, 4 legs on a table, 5 fingers on a hand, etc.). Have students pick an item from the list and figure out how many there would be if the items were doubled. Have each student draw a picture and write a number sentence for a class doubles book (see Figure 5.2).

Holey Doubles   Give each student a piece of paper and have them fold it in half. Students pick a 1–10 number card (see CD) and, with the paper folded,

Figure 5.2 *This page for the class doubles book describes the legs on 2 horses.*

use a handheld paper punch to punch that number of holes in their paper. Students then open the folded paper to reveal double the holes. Students record the doubles number sentence on their paper and write a doubles story about their holes (i.e., "There were 5 spiders and 5 more crawled in. How many were there?"). Students can get creative and decorate around the holes to make them look like flowers or spiders or lollipops or suns. The doubles art can be posted on a bulletin board to display a variety of doubles equations as in Figure 5.3.

Figure 5.3 *Four holes are punched on the outside of the folded paper to reveal double the holes when the paper is opened. Students can decorate the holes to look like spiders and add a doubles number sentence.*

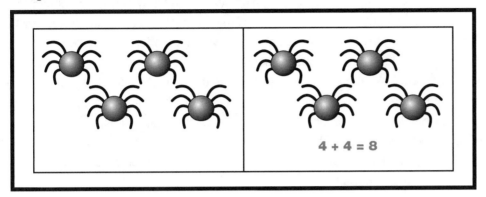

4 + 4 = 8

Building Automaticity

Targeted Practice

Individualized Fact Card Practice Referring to each student's Fact Check will allow you to select specific fact cards that meet her needs. Are there specific doubles facts that this student struggles to recall? Practice with targeted facts allows for more repetition of those facts and narrows the scope of the task for each student. Students can be given the job of finding their "focus facts" in their deck of fact cards before beginning a focused fact card practice.

A Fact Card Menu Fact cards (see CD) can be a source of activities that students do independently at school or at home. The following activities alleviate the stress that is sometimes associated with fact cards as they emphasize knowledge of the answer rather than speed. Suggest one of the following for students who need additional practice with the facts.

Doubles Fact Cards—Addition			
0 + 0	1 + 1	2 + 2	3 + 3
4 + 4	5 + 5	6 + 6	7 + 7
8 + 8	9 + 9	10 +10	

- Pick a card and draw a picture to show the fact.
- Pick an addition fact card and write a subtraction fact that goes with it.
- Pick a card and write the fact three times.
- Pick a card and write a story problem for the fact.
- Pick a card and show the fact on a number line. Record the number sentence by the number line.

The Teacher's Role During Game Time   While students play games, you might either observe their play or capitalize on your opportunity to work with a small group of students. Watching students as they play games allows you to gain insights about their fluency with math facts. You will quickly identify those who have mastered facts and those who need additional support.

Although those observations are extremely helpful, it might also be beneficial to take the opportunity to address the needs of specific students. As most students are developing their rapid recall of facts through the games, you might conduct small-group assessments, lead intervention groups, or conduct individual interviews. Think about both assessment and instruction as you balance opportunities to observe students at play and support students individually or in small groups.

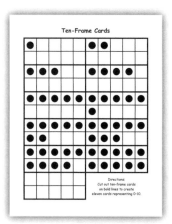

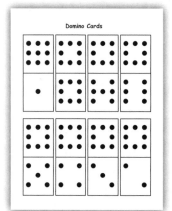

Double Ten-Frames   Provide each pair with two sets of ten-frame cards (see CD) containing frames with 0–10 dots. Have students work with partners to find doubles (i.e., locate the frames with 6 dots on each frame), find the sums, and record the number sentences.

I Spy Doubles   Have students search for double dominoes, dominoes with the same number of dots on each side, and write matching addition equations (see Figure 5.4). See the CD for domino templates.

Figure 5.4 *These students search for double dominoes.*

1	9	5
4	3	6
7	8	2

Figure 5.5 *Tossing beanbags at a number chart on the floor, and doubling the number the bag lands on, incorporates movement into math facts practice.*

Beanbag Addition   Create a floor mat with a white shower curtain liner or large poster board, marking nine sections, each containing a number from 1–9 (see Figure 5.5). Students take turns tossing a beanbag and calling out the number it lands on and the double. Students record their double equations.

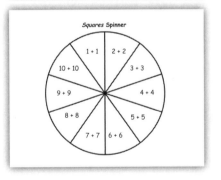

Squares   The goal of *Squares* is to be the first player to have markers on four numbers that form a square on the game board. Students play with partners. Each pair needs a *Squares* spinner and game board (see CD) along with game markers (e.g., beans or counters). Players take turns spinning, finding the sum, and placing their marker on the board. The first player to have four markers arranged to form a square is the winner. For a noncompetitive option, have partners work together to spin, add, and cover doubles sums, talking together about where to place each marker as they try to form a square. When a square is formed, students clear the board and start again.

Doubles Memory   In *Doubles Memory*, students try to match a doubles fact card (5 + 5) with the correct sum (10). Students work in pairs and spread the cards (see CD) facedown on a desk, table, or floor. Each player takes turns choosing two cards. If the cards go together (the doubles fact and the sum), the player keeps the cards and gets another turn. If the cards do not match, the player returns them to the same spot on the desk, facedown, and his turn is over. The player with the most cards at the end of the game is the winner.

Monitoring Progress

Individual Teacher-Guided Fact Checks   Individual student assessment might be indicated for students who have extreme difficulty with the cumulative Fact Checks. Using a set of fact cards, assess the child's fluency verbally, beginning with simpler facts and then moving to those that are causing difficulty. As a child misses, set the card aside. When a child misses five facts, stop and set a goal for those facts. Give the missed fact cards to the student, discuss any strategies that might help them better remember those facts, and determine a time frame for when you will recheck for mastery of the facts.

Tip   Many students have difficulty with timed tests. Teacher-administered oral fact checks provide a clear picture of fact mastery.

Connecting to Subtraction

As students develop an understanding of doubles facts, take every opportunity to talk about the connection between addition and subtraction facts. Discussing halves will demonstrate the inverse of doubles and show what happens when one half is separated from the other—the same amount always remains. The two addends in a doubles number sentence can be thought of as halves. Thinking *halves* simplifies finding the difference for doubles subtraction.

Literature Link: *Martha Blah Blah*

In *Martha Blah Blah* (1996) by Susan Meddaugh, a dog gains the ability to speak when eating alphabet soup but encounters problems when half of the letters are removed from the soup.

Before Reading   Have students turn and tell a partner what they think dogs might say if they could speak. Share a few of their ideas. Tell students you will be reading a story about a dog who speaks. Before you begin reading, have students recite the alphabet as you record the letters on chart paper or the board. Count the total number of letters in the alphabet and record *26* on the board.

During Reading   After reading that Granny Flo removed half of the letters, pause to identify and cross off the letters she removed. Ask students to predict if she removed more than, less than, or about half of the letters.

After Reading   Ask students if the 13 letters removed were half of the alphabet. Give partners 26 counters to represent the letters. Have students explain how they know that 13 is half of 26.

Prepare bowls of cereal letters, or magnetic letters, to represent bowls of alphabet soup. Have bowls with the following amounts of letters: 2, 4, 6, 8, 10, 12, 14, 16, 18, and 20. The actual letters in each bowl do not matter, just the quantity of letters in the bowls. Have students work in pairs or groups to count the letters in their bowls and then remove half of the letters like Granny Flo did. Students must find out how many letters are left in their bowls and record the subtraction number sentence on the *Letters in Our Soup* recording sheet (see CD) as in Figure 5.6. As students finish, have them switch bowls with another group and do it several more times.

After students have worked with several bowls of soup, have students share, as you record, the different number sentences for half of the letters. Once you have completed the subtraction number sentences, write associated doubles addition sentences next to the subtraction sentences. Ask students to describe how the addition and subtraction sentences are the same and how they are different. Their comments will likely include:

They have the same numbers in them, but in different places.

They all have 2 numbers that are the same and 1 that is different.

If you take a half away, you get the other half.

Figure 5.6 *This student explores subtraction by removing half of the letters from his soup.*

Letters in Our Soup

Letters in the bowl	How many would be left if we took half away?	Number sentence
14	7	$14 - 7 = 7$ 7 letters left
10	5	$10 - 5 = 5$ 5 letters left
16	8	$16 - 8 = 8$ 8 letters left

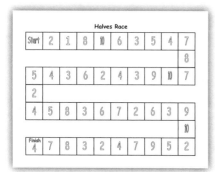

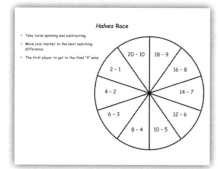

Or students might use the *Are Doubles and Halves the Same?* recording sheet on the CD to explore the similarities and differences between addition and subtraction doubles facts as in Figure 5.7.

Practicing for Fluency

Halves Race   In *Halves Race*, students spin and subtract in order to move along the game board. Each pair need one *Halves Race* game board, a doubles subtraction spinner (see CD), and game markers. Students take turns spinning, finding the difference, and moving to the next space containing that difference on the board. The first player to the finish wins.

Figure 5.7 *Students gain insights when they are asked to observe math facts.*

Are Doubles and Halves the Same?

Complete each number sentence.

1 + 1 = __2__	2 − 1 = __1__
2 + 2 = __4__	4 − 2 = __2__
3 + 3 = __6__	6 − 3 = __3__
4 + 4 = __8__	8 − 4 = __4__
5 + 5 = __10__	10 − 5 = __5__
6 + 6 = __12__	12 − 6 = __6__
7 + 7 = __14__	14 − 7 = __7__
8 + 8 = __16__	16 − 8 = __8__
9 + 9 = __18__	18 − 9 = __9__
10 + 10 = __20__	20 − 10 = __10__

doubles   halves

What do you notice about the two stacks of number sentences?

One colimn is doubles the other is halves there just opposits

---

Halves Memory   In *Halves Memory*, students try to match a doubles subtraction fact card (10 – 5) with the correct difference (5). Students work in pairs and spread the cards (see CD) facedown on a desk, table, or floor. Each player takes turns choosing two cards. If the cards go together (the subtraction fact and the difference), the player keeps the cards and gets another turn. If the cards do not match, the player returns them to the same spot on the desk, facedown, and her turn is over. The player with the most cards at the end of the game is the winner.

Which Sign?   *Which Sign?* provides a review of doubles addition and subtraction facts and builds foundational algebra skills as students explore building equations. Partners work to complete the *Which Sign?* recording sheet (see CD), deciding if an addition or subtraction sign would make the equation true (i.e., Would + or – complete the number sentences 6 ☐ 6 = 12 or 16 ☐ 8 = 8?). Rather than making copies of the worksheet for each student, consider putting it in a plastic sleeve and placing it at a center. Students then copy each equation on a blank paper, inserting the sign they choose. Asking students to write about how they made their decision gives insight into their thinking. How did they know where to place an addition sign or subtraction sign?

Halves Memory Cards

0 – 0	2 – 1	4 – 2
6 – 3	8 – 4	10 – 5
12 – 6	14 – 7	16 – 8
18 – 9	20 –10	

Halves Memory Cards

0	1	2
3	4	5
6	7	8
9	10	

Name: _____

Which Sign?

Which sign makes each number sentence true?
Place + or – where it belongs.

14 ☐ 7 = 7   10 ☐ 5 = 5

3 ☐ 3 = 6   4 ☐ 4 = 8

5 ☐ 5 = 10   6 ☐ 6 = 12

12 ☐ 6 = 6   7 ☐ 7 = 14

18 ☐ 9 = 9   16 ☐ 8 = 8

8 ☐ 8 = 16   10 ☐ 10 = 20

4 ☐ 2 = 2   9 ☐ 9 = 18

How did you know when to use an addition sign?
_____
_____
_____

CHAPTER SIX

Making 10

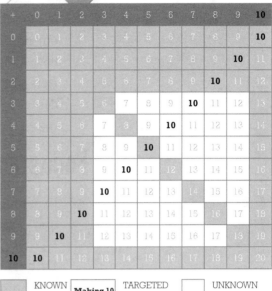

+	0	1	2	3	4	5	6	7	8	9	**10**
0	0	1	2	3	4	5	6	7	8	9	**10**
1	1	2	3	4	5	6	7	8	9	**10**	11
2	2	3	4	5	6	7	8	9	**10**	11	12
3	3	4	5	6	7	8	9	**10**	11	12	13
4	4	5	6	7	8	9	**10**	11	12	13	14
5	5	6	7	8	9	**10**	11	12	13	14	15
6	6	7	8	9	**10**	11	12	13	14	15	16
7	7	8	9	**10**	11	12	13	14	15	16	17
8	8	9	**10**	11	12	13	14	15	16	17	18
9	9	**10**	11	12	13	14	15	16	17	18	19
10	**10**	11	12	13	14	15	16	17	18	19	20

KNOWN FACTS **Making 10** TARGETED FACTS UNKNOWN FACTS

Our students have now examined +0, +1, +2, +10, and doubles facts. They have explored the concepts, developed strategies, and are working toward automaticity with these facts. Although some strategies, like counting on, worked well as we introduced +1 and +2 facts, they are not efficient as we move to larger addends. When faced with finding the sum of 6 + 6, students could count on from 6, but it would be quite cumbersome, so we introduced the more efficient strategy of thinking doubles. Our goal is that students build a repertoire of

strategies so they are able to move to more efficient methods as they build a stronger understanding of numbers. We continue to expose students to varied ways of thinking about numbers so they can access the most efficient methods and build their number sense as they work toward fluency.

Our next set of facts is grounded in one of the most significant ideas about our number system—it is a system of tens. Knowing the addition facts that have a sum of 10 provides the underpinning for knowing many other addition facts. Developing a strong understanding and automatic recall of tens facts deserves significant focus.

Focusing on the Big Ideas

Exploring big ideas about mathematics provides the backdrop for our exploration of making tens. Following are some big ideas.

Our number system is a system of tens.

Our number system is a base-ten system. Students have worked with numbers organized in tens as they explore ten-frames and hundred charts. The understanding of tens allows them to understand place value. And their automatic recall of number combinations that make ten allows them to efficiently do mental math computations.

The order of the addends does not change the sum (the commutative property).

The knowledge of this property is becoming more significant as students continue their goal to master 0–10 facts. Our initial thought is that there will be eleven facts in this set, but by the time we introduce *making ten* as a strategy, students already have knowledge of 0 + 10, 1 + 9, 2 + 8, 5 + 5, 8 + 2, 9 + 1, and 10 + 0, which leaves only four facts to focus on: 3 + 7, 4 + 6, and 6 + 4, 7 + 3, as illustrated in the addition chart at the beginning of this chapter. And again, with understanding that the order of the addends does not matter, the targeted facts are further reduced to two facts: 3 + 7 and 4 + 6.

Addition and subtraction are inverse operations.

If students know two addends that make ten (e.g., 4 + 6), an understanding that addition and subtraction are inverse operations will help them find the difference of 10 − 6 or 10 − 4. Automatic recall of facts that make ten supports recall of the related subtraction facts.

Key questions related to the big ideas for making ten are:

Does the order of the addends affect the sum? Give examples to justify your thinking.

Is there a connection between 2 + 8 and 3 + 7? What connection do you see? Does it make sense?

If you know one part and the whole is 10, how will you find the other part?

Our goal is to continually reinforce the big ideas related to math facts as we help students develop addition and subtraction strategies.

Understanding Making Ten

Literature Link: *Ten Apples up on Top!*

In *Ten Apples up on Top!* (1961) by Dr. Seuss, writing as Theo LeSieg, a lion, a tiger, and a dog have fun balancing different amounts of apples until they are finally all able to balance 10 apples on their heads. Through this story, students explore different combinations that make ten.

Before Reading Ask students if they have ever tried to balance something on their heads. Have them turn to a partner and share an item that might be easy to balance and an item that might be hard to balance. Make a two-column chart on the board with headings Easy and Hard and list a few of the items they mention. Ask students where they would put apples. Would they be easy to balance or hard? Why? Tell students you will be reading a story about animals that balance apples on their heads. Ask them to listen to see if it is easy or hard for these animals.

During Reading Occasionally ask students how many more apples an animal would need to have 10 apples balanced on his head. There is no need to wait for students to do the computations. Simply allow them to begin predicting quantities and listen for the reasonableness of their predictions.

After Reading Ask students if the story events could really happen. Would it be possible for these animals to balance 10 apples as they jump rope, or climb trees, or run through town? Acknowledge that even though it is not a true story, it is fun to think about balancing all of those apples.

Tell students that they will be imagining that they are balancing 10 apples on their heads, but not just juicy red apples, they might also have some bright yellow apples. Tell students that you are wondering how many of the 10 apples are red and how many are yellow. Have students fold a piece of paper into three columns, or use the *Apples on Top* recording sheet on the CD to find some different possibilities of red and yellow apples in a stack of 10 (see Figure 6.1). Have students work with partners to find some possibilities. Give each pair of students 10 two-color counters, with red on one side and yellow on the other side, to represent the apples. Students use their counters to find a possibility, write the numbers in the columns (number of red and number of yellow), and then record an addition number sentence in the last column.

After students have found some different combinations of red and yellow apples in the stack, have partners share their possibilities with the class. As

Figure 6.1 *This student explores possible combinations of red and yellow apples in a stack of 10.*

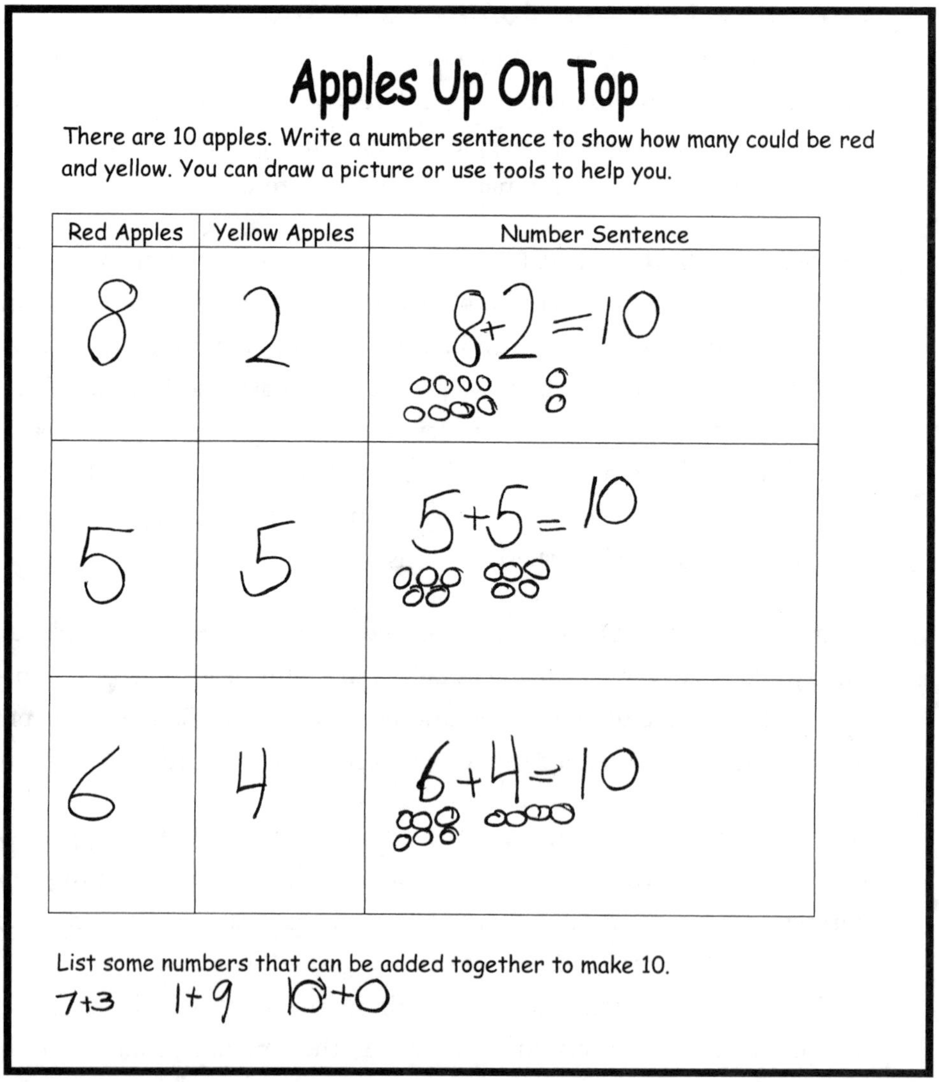

Apples Up On Top

There are 10 apples. Write a number sentence to show how many could be red and yellow. You can draw a picture or use tools to help you.

Red Apples	Yellow Apples	Number Sentence
8	2	$8 + 2 = 10$
5	5	$5 + 5 = 10$
6	4	$6 + 4 = 10$

List some numbers that can be added together to make 10.

7+3   1+9   10+0

partners share a combination of 10, record the number sentence on the board or chart paper. Students will probably give combinations in random order. This is a great opportunity to encourage organized thinking. You might ask:

> *Did we get them all?*
>
> *Did we miss any?*
>
> *Did we say something twice?*
>
> *Is this list confusing?*
>
> *Can we organize it so it is easier to see?*

Reorganize the data beginning with 0 red and 10 yellow, moving through the data in a systematic way from 0–10 red apples, then ask students if the data are easier to see. Did they miss anything? Do they have all of the possibilities? Now, ask them what they notice about the number sentences. Insights will likely include:

> *They all add up to 10.*
>
> *There is a 0 and 10 and a 10 and 0. There's a 1 and 9 and a 9 and 1.*
>
> *Every two numbers has a flip-flopped set.*
>
> *The number of red apples goes up 1 each time.*
>
> *The number of yellow apples goes down 1 each time.*
>
> *Each time you add a red apple, you take away a yellow apple.*

Ask students if any of the facts look familiar. Have they studied them before (e.g., 10 + 0, 9 + 1, 8 + 2, or 5 + 5)? Have students fold a paper into two columns and label them I Know Them and My New Facts, then make a list of the making-ten facts they already know and the making-ten facts they still need to learn.

Exploring the Facts: The Cupcake Problem

Ten-frames are the ideal visual for the making-ten strategy. The ten-frame template organizes 10 as two sets of 5. As counters are placed in the sections of the ten-frame, students can quickly determine the number of sections with counters and the number without counters to visualize the two addends that have a sum of 10. Ten-frames, accompanying the following problem, allow students to explore the solution in a hands-on way.

> Rita has a pan for 10 cupcakes. She wants to put cherry and lemon cupcakes in the pan. What are some different amounts of cherry and lemon cupcakes she can put in the pan?

Provide each student with a ten-frame template to represent the pan (see CD) and 10 two-color counters to represent the cherry and lemon cupcakes. Have students work with partners to find number sentences that make ten by placing red counters (cherry cupcakes) in sections of the frame and then filling the remaining sections with yellow counters (lemon cupcakes). Have students record the number sentences as they explore them with their counters and frames. After allowing some time for investigation, have students share some of the cupcake possibilities. Record the making-ten number sentences on the board as they share their ideas.

As you record the number sentences, ask students to observe for patterns. Do they see the different order of addends, the commutative property (e.g., 3 + 7 and 7 + 3)? Do they notice that as we increase one type of cupcake, the other type decreases (e.g., 3 + 7 and 4 + 6)? Ask questions to guide students to an understanding of the flexibility of numbers—there are multiple ways to make ten.

Once students have explored and discussed cupcake possibilities, give each pair a set of 0–10 ten-frame cards (see CD). Have them shuffle the cards and take turns pulling a card, saying the number it represents, and telling how many more would be needed to make ten. Observe students as they work in pairs, to assess who might need to work in a small group to further explore the concept and who is ready for practice tasks to move toward automatic recall of the facts.

Supporting All Learners

The following classroom activities provide you with additional lesson ideas for the whole class or for small teacher-led groups with students who might need to explore making ten in a different way.

> **Tip** Using two-color counters allows students to quickly see the two addends that have a sum of 10. If two-color counters are not available, simply use 10 counters and have students place some counters in the sections of the ten-frame. Students then record the number of counters on the frame and the number of sections with no counters to build their equations.

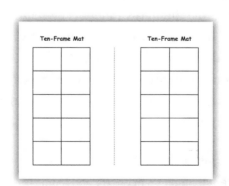

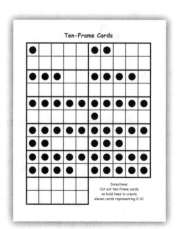

Student Lineups   Gather 10 students to line up in front of the class. Have students identify how many boys and girls are in the group. Record the number sentence. Invite a different group to line up, identify the number of boys and girls, and record the number sentence. Ask students to turn and share two other boy/girl combinations that would make a group of 10.

Exploring with Bead Counters   Bead counters are a simple-to-make, hands-on tool that engage students and help them visualize tens. Make simple bead counters, or have students make them, by placing colored beads on a pipe cleaner. Beads should be placed so there are five of one color and then five of a different color on the pipe cleaner, then the ends of the pipe cleaner are bent so the beads will not fall off (see Figure 6.2). Be sure to allow room to move the beads along the pipe cleaner.

Begin by posing some questions to assess students' readiness level.

How many beads are on your pipe cleaner? How do you know?
(probably counted)

Move 5 beads of the same color to one side of your bead counter.

How many beads did I move? How do you know?

Can they immediately state that there are 5 beads? Do they know that 5 is half of 10? Move 6 beads to the side, 5 of the same color and 1 of a different color.

How many beads are to the side now? How do you know?

Are they using their understanding of 5 to determine that 1 more is 6? Show 7 beads, 5 of the same color and 2 of a different color.

How many beads are to the side now? How do you know?

Tip   When exploring making-ten facts, every fact has a sum of 10. The challenge with this set of facts is to recognize the addend pairs that make ten. Try some missing addend equations to strengthen students' recognition of these pairs.

$$4 + \underline{\hspace{1cm}} = 10$$
$$\underline{\hspace{1cm}} + 7 = 10$$

Figure 6.2 *Bead counters are created with ten beads, five beads each of two different colors.*

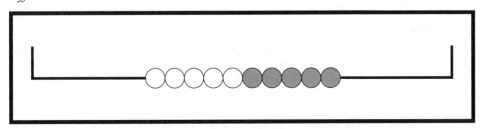

Once you have a sense for students' understanding of the numbers they are seeing, cover some beads with your hand and ask students to tell you how many are hiding, or how many more you would need to make ten.

Cover 5.

How many are hiding? How many more would I need to make ten?

Uncover and check their predictions.

Cover 6.

How many are hiding? How many more would I need to make ten?

Uncover and check their predictions.

Have students use their bead counters to perform the following tasks and answer the following questions.

Show me 6. Can you do it without counting? Explain how you knew without counting.

Show me 9. Can you do it without counting? Explain how you knew without counting.

Show me 4. Can you do it without counting? Explain how you knew without counting.

Push the 10 beads together. Pull 5 to the side. *How many more do you need to make ten? How do you know? How would we write that number sentence?*

Push the 10 beads together. Pull 1 to the side. *How many more do you need to make ten? How do you know? How would we write that number sentence?*

Push the 10 beads together. Pull 3 to the side. *How many more do you need to make ten? How do you know? How would we write that number sentence?*

Tip As we work toward fluency with basic math facts, we take every opportunity to extend students' strategic thinking. As students become skilled at strategies like making ten, asking them how the strategy could help them with 20 + 80 or 40 + 60 will stimulate and extend their thinking about numbers.

Continue posing similar problems and observing students as they explore making ten with their bead counters.

Allow students to use their bead counters as manipulatives for interactive games that focus on the making-ten strategy. The bead counters will allow them to check their answers or find solutions when they are unsure. Bead counter activities can also be placed in classroom centers. Students might draw a 0–10 number card, use their bead counters to find the other addend that would make ten, and then record the number sentence (see Figure 6.3).

Figure 6.3 *Bead counters allow students to visualize making ten.*

Building Automaticity

Once students have explored the concept of making ten and observed and discussed patterns, it is time for repeated practice to develop automatic recall of the facts.

Targeted Practice

Ongoing Interactive Practice Automaticity with math facts requires practice. Activities, games, and fact card activities provide a multitude of ways for students to practice their facts. Ongoing practice is critical. Practice should take place on a daily basis while students are learning their facts. And, to retain their facts, ongoing practice continues to be necessary.

Practice can take place during math class or at other times during the school day (i.e., teachers might make games available as students arrive to school in the morning). Many teachers insert quick fact reviews into their lessons on a regular basis. Even a five-minute activity provides repeated exposure to the targeted skills and promotes fluency. Some teachers schedule opportunities several times a week (i.e., ten minutes on Monday, Wednesday, and Friday) for students to play math fact games while the teacher works with students who need additional support with their math facts. Even indoor recess provides an opportunity for students to play math games.

Practice can happen at home, too. Offering a menu of home ideas for using fact cards can help parents identify effective ways to support their children at home. Identifying and sending home specific fact cards will ensure that students get practice with the needed facts. See the parent letter on the CD, which provides ideas for home practice as well as an explanation for going beyond speed and memory when addressing math facts with their children. Students can use a fact log (see CD) to record when they practice, how long they practice, and the targeted facts. Ongoing opportunities for students to practice math facts promote math fact fluency.

Domino Tens   Provide students with a set of dominoes or create dominoes by copying the domino template (see CD) on card stock paper. Students search for dominoes that have a total of 10 dots and write the corresponding addition equations (e.g., a domino with 4 dots on one side and 6 dots on the other side is represented by $4 + 6 = 10$ and $6 + 4 = 10$).

Fact Card Problems   Have students work with partners to pick a making-ten fact card. Students then write a word problem to go with the fact and draw a picture to show the fact (i.e., for $3 + 7$, students write "There were 3 white dogs and 7 brown dogs. How many dogs were there?").

Fact Card Ten-Frames   Have students select a fact card and show the fact by placing two-color counters on a ten-frame (see CD). One addend is represented by red counters and the other by yellow counters.

Making Ten at a Math Fact Center   Provide ongoing practice with the making-ten strategy through center activities.

Tip Mixed Fact Card Reviews

When working with fact cards for the making-ten strategy, the sum for all of the fact cards will be 10. Rather than conducting reviews with only making-ten fact cards, which results in the same answer for every card, mix in fact cards from previously learned fact sets to provide a comprehensive review. This challenges students to recall the addend pairs that make ten.

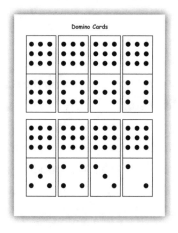

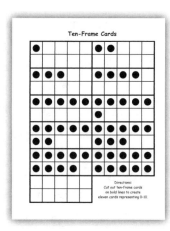

- Place some bead counters and fact cards at the center and have students select a fact card, model it with a bead counter, and then write the number sentence for the fact.

- Place some bead counters at the center and challenge students to find number sentences with a sum of 10 using the bead counters. Have them record their equations as in Figure 6.4.

- Give students number sentences with a missing addend and have them use counters and ten-frames to find the missing addend as in Figure 6.5.

These activities are simple, require few materials, and provide ongoing exposure to making-ten facts.

Fact Sorting   Sorting is an engaging fact card review activity. Students are given assorted sets of fact cards and asked to work with partners to sort the fact cards and then to explain their sorting. Do they recognize facts that make ten or doubles or +1/+2 facts? Students receive repeated exposure to the facts as they work to sort their fact cards in a way that makes sense to them.

Figure 6.4 *This student was able to find many equations with a sum of 10 by using bead counters.*

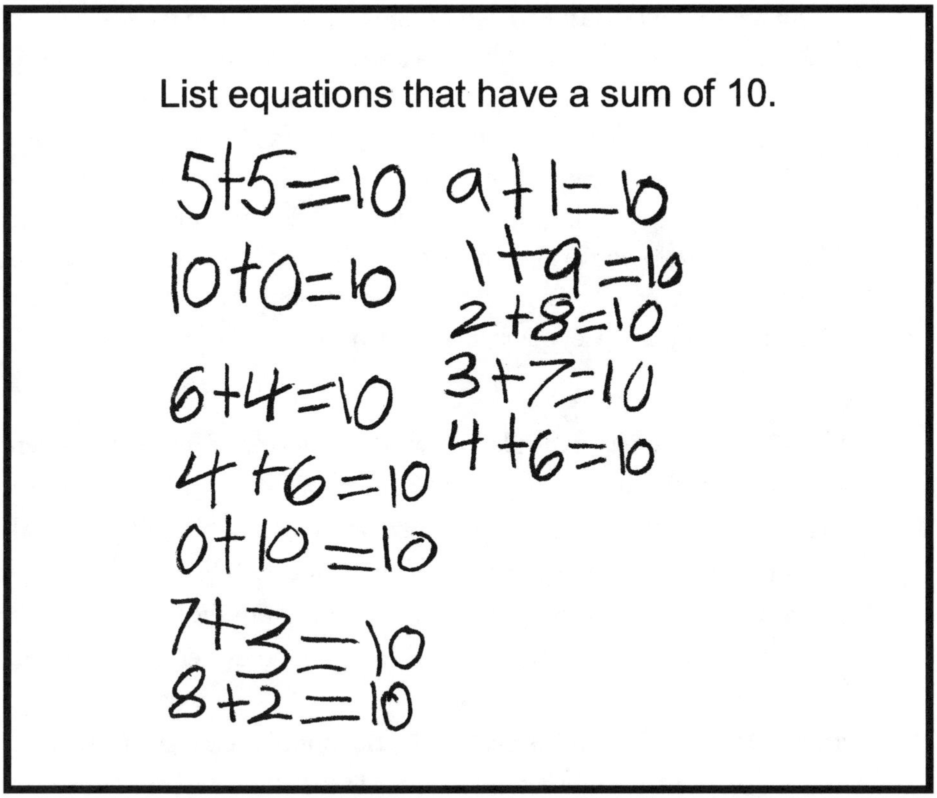

List equations that have a sum of 10.

$$5+5=10 \quad 9+1=10$$
$$10+0=10 \quad 1+9=10$$
$$2+8=10$$
$$6+4=10 \quad 3+7=10$$
$$4+6=10 \quad 4+6=10$$
$$0+10=10$$
$$7+3=10$$
$$8+2=10$$

Figure 6.5 *Finding missing addends by using ten-frames is a simple center task.*

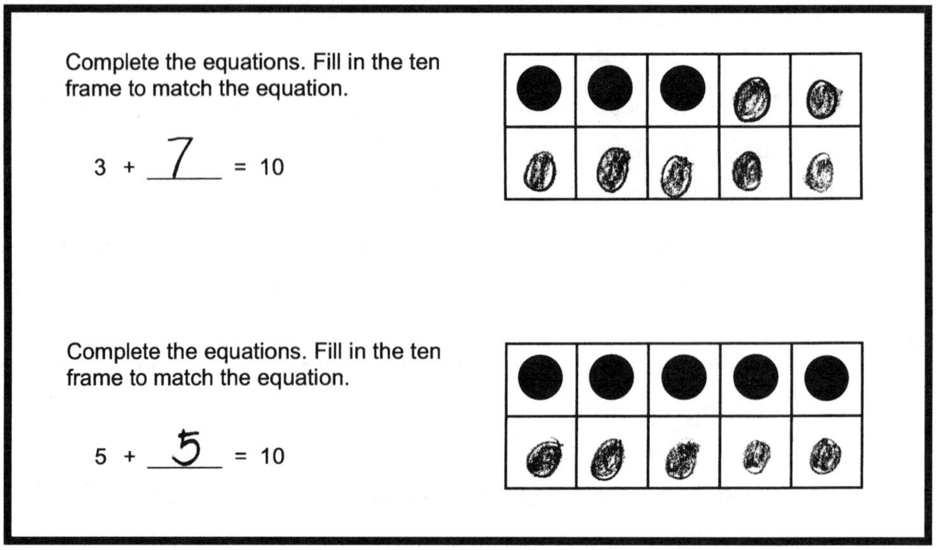

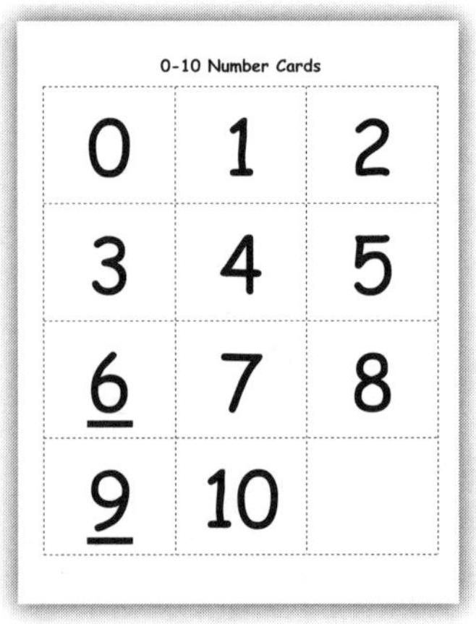

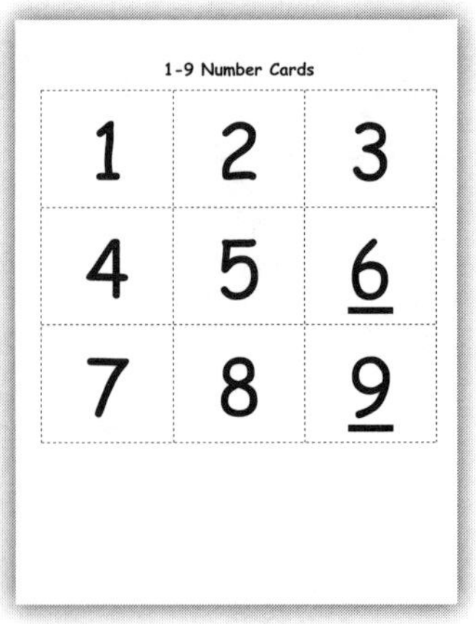

Complete the equations. Fill in the ten frame to match the equation.

3 + __7__ = 10

Complete the equations. Fill in the ten frame to match the equation.

5 + __5__ = 10

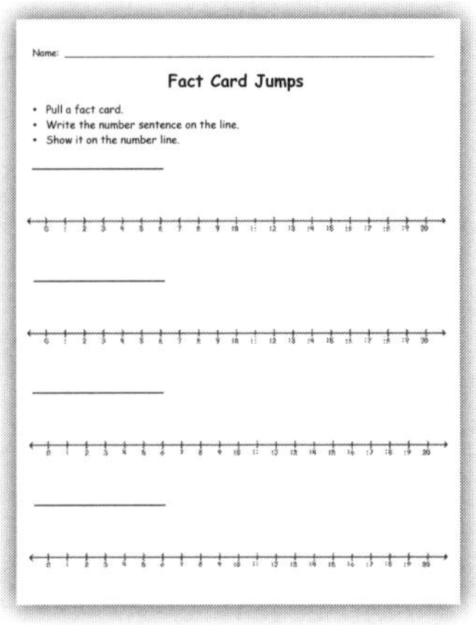

Fact Card Jumps Remember to adapt activities from previous chapters for each new set of math facts. *Fact Card Jumps* (see CD) was introduced as students explored +1/+2 facts. For making tens, have students select a fact card and show the fact with jumps on a number line. Be sure to have students write the number sentence by their number line.

Focus on Mastery Rather Than Speed As we explore the teaching of math facts, we have begun to rethink some traditional classroom games played with fact cards. To alleviate anxiety and ensure that the students who need the fact practice stay engaged, we recommend fact card activities that do not eliminate those students who struggle with facts because they are most needy of the practice. In addition, speed competitions (e.g., one student pitted against another) generally end in frustration for the students who need the practice provided by the activity. Fact card activities that ensure continued involvement of all students best meet our instructional goals.

Make Ten *Make Ten* can be played by two or more students, with students trying to find cards that have a sum of 10. Four sets of 0–10 cards (see CD) are needed to play the game. Players lay 16 cards face up in a 4 × 4 grid. Players work with a partner to remove *tens* (e.g., a 4 and 6 or a 2 and 8). When cards are removed from the 4 × 4 grid, they are replaced with cards from the deck. Students work together to remove as many tens as possible before they get stuck (no tens left).

Fish for Ten *Fish for Ten* is played like the popular card game, *Go Fish*, with a making-ten twist. Four sets of 1–9 cards (see CD) are needed to play the game; however, removing the tens and face cards from a standard deck of playing cards will also create a set of cards that is perfect for this game. Seven cards are dealt to each player. On a turn, a player asks for a specific card they need to make a 10. For example, Brendan has a 3, so he asks Allison if she has a 7. Allison must give a 7 if she has one. If not, she says "Go fish." Brendan then draws the top card from the draw pile. If he happens to draw the card he asked for, he shows it to Allison and the other players, places his 10 (3 and 7 cards) in a pile, faceup, in front of him, and takes another turn. However, if he draws a card that is not what he asked for, his turn is over and the next player begins his turn. *Fish for Ten* continues until either someone has no cards left in their hand or the draw pile runs out. The winner is the player who has collected the most tens (card combinations with a sum of 10).

Fill Ten   In *Fill Ten*, each player begins by placing 0–9 beans, or small counters, on each of six ten-frames on their game board (see CD). The goal is for students to spin the number that will complete each frame (i.e., if 4 beans are on a frame the student would need to spin a 6 to complete it). Players take turns spinning a 1–10 spinner and, if possible, adding that number of beans to complete one of their frames. If a number is spun that does not complete a frame, that player loses his turn. The first to fill all six ten-frames wins.

> **Talking About Facts**   Many students retain facts more readily if they verbalize the facts. Rather than simply looking at facts and "doing them in their head," encourage students to verbalize as they play math games. Each time they repeat the math fact, they are working on committing that fact to memory. In addition, when math facts are verbalized, partners are more likely to catch each other's errors. And in math games, it is important that partners know what each other is thinking. Silent games, in which students simply place a marker on a number, can leave one partner wondering what the other has done. Encourage students to talk as they think about math facts.

> **Tip**   For all games, decide on the rules that work for you. Many traditional games, like *Go Fish*, are played differently by different people. Modify any of the directions to make these games work with your time limits, available resources, and the ability levels of your students. There is no one right way to play a math fact game. Be creative and vary the game to suit your needs.
>
> Many activities do not have winners or losers; they are simply interactive activities that generate talk and provide repeated practice with specific sets of math facts.

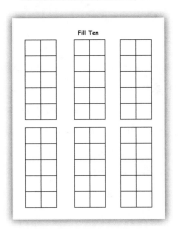

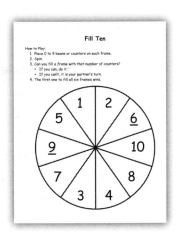

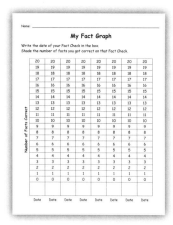

Monitoring Progress

Graphing Progress Each time students complete a Fact Check for a specific set of facts (e.g., making ten), have them color in sections on their own progress graph (see CD), showing the number of facts they knew. The graph provides a quick visual of their progress.

Celebrating Success Keep pulling out those addition charts on which students record their known facts. They have come a long way in their goal to master addition and subtraction facts!

+	0	1	2	3	4	5	6	7	8	9	10
0	0	1	2	3	4	5	6	7	8	9	10
1	1	2	3	4	5	6	7	8	9	10	11
2	2	3	4	5	6	7	8	9	10	11	12
3	3	4	5	6				10			13
4	4	5	6		8		10				14
5	5	6	7			10					15
6	6	7	8		10		12				16
7	7	8	9	10				14			17
8	8	9	10						16		18
9	9	10	11							18	19
10	10	11	12	13	14	15	16	17	18	19	20

This is a great point to spend a little extra time on automaticity practice. The facts that students have now explored provide them with clues to the facts that are coming next. Students will soon see how they can use their knowledge of doubles and making tens to find the sums of near-doubles and near-ten facts. The more fluent students are with these facts, the easier the next fact sets will be.

Attending to Anxiety Observe students for signs of anxiety before and during Fact Checks. Are there students who get anxious as soon as a Fact Check is mentioned? High anxiety might indicate the need to modify the Fact Check by decreasing the number of facts (e.g., ten facts) or allowing the student additional time to complete the task. Once the student experiences success, more facts can be added or the time can be decreased.

Connecting to Subtraction

As students develop an understanding of making ten, take every opportunity to talk about the connection between addition and subtraction facts.

Exploring Subtraction: Revisiting *Ten Apples up on Top!*

In *Ten Apples up on Top!* (1961), Dr. Seuss tells the story of three animals that have adventures through town while balancing apples on their heads. When they finally get 10 apples balanced on their heads, they are determined not to let any of them drop. This story sets a perfect context for the concept of subtraction from 10 as we explore what might happen if apples fall from their heads.

Before Reading   Show the book cover and ask students to turn and tell a partner something they remember about the story. Remind students that the animals were so pleased when they finally got 10 apples balanced on their heads, but that there were times when we thought some apples might fall. Tell them you will be rereading (or doing a picture walk and retelling) the story. Have them listen for what might have caused the apples to drop.

During Reading   Reread the story or remind students of the events in the story through a picture walk and retelling of the story.

After Reading   Ask students to identify some things that might have caused apples to drop (e.g., the mother bear chasing them with a broom, the birds trying to eat them, the baby bear chasing them with a tennis racket). Tell students you will be writing number sentences to show what might have happened if some apples had dropped. Gather some linking cubes and count as you place 10 cubes in a stack to represent the apples on the tiger's head. Using 5 cubes of one color and then 5 cubes of another color will help students visualize amounts as you begin to remove cubes. Ask students to turn and tell a partner how many apples will be left if 1 apple fell off the tiger's head. Take 1 cube off the stack. Students should be able to immediately know that there will be 9 apples left, either from their counting back experiences or from their mastery of −1 facts. Ask students to turn and share the number sentence that shows the subtraction fact. Record *10 − 1 = 9.*

Give each pair of students a set of 10 linking cubes (5 of one color and 5 of another color) and have them connect them to make a stack of 10 to represent the 10 apples balanced on the tiger's head. Guiding students to build their stack with 5 cubes of one color and then the 5 of the other color results in a better visual of *10* as they remove cubes. Give students a copy of the *Dropping Apples* recording sheet, or have them fold a paper into three columns labeled Total Apples, Apples Dropped, and Apples Left. Tell students they will be drawing a card from a 0–10 deck (see CD) to see how many apples dropped off the tiger's head. Remind students to always start with 10 cubes for the 10 apples. Observe as students draw a card, record the number that dropped, remove cubes from their stack, and record the subtraction number sentence to show how many apples are left as in Figure 6.6.

After repeating this several times, have the class members share and discuss their findings. Record the number sentences on the board for each amount of apples dropped. Ask students what they notice about the subtraction number sentences. Have them turn and tell a partner how thinking about making ten can help someone subtract from 10.

Figure 6.6 *Students explore subtraction through a story-based problem.*

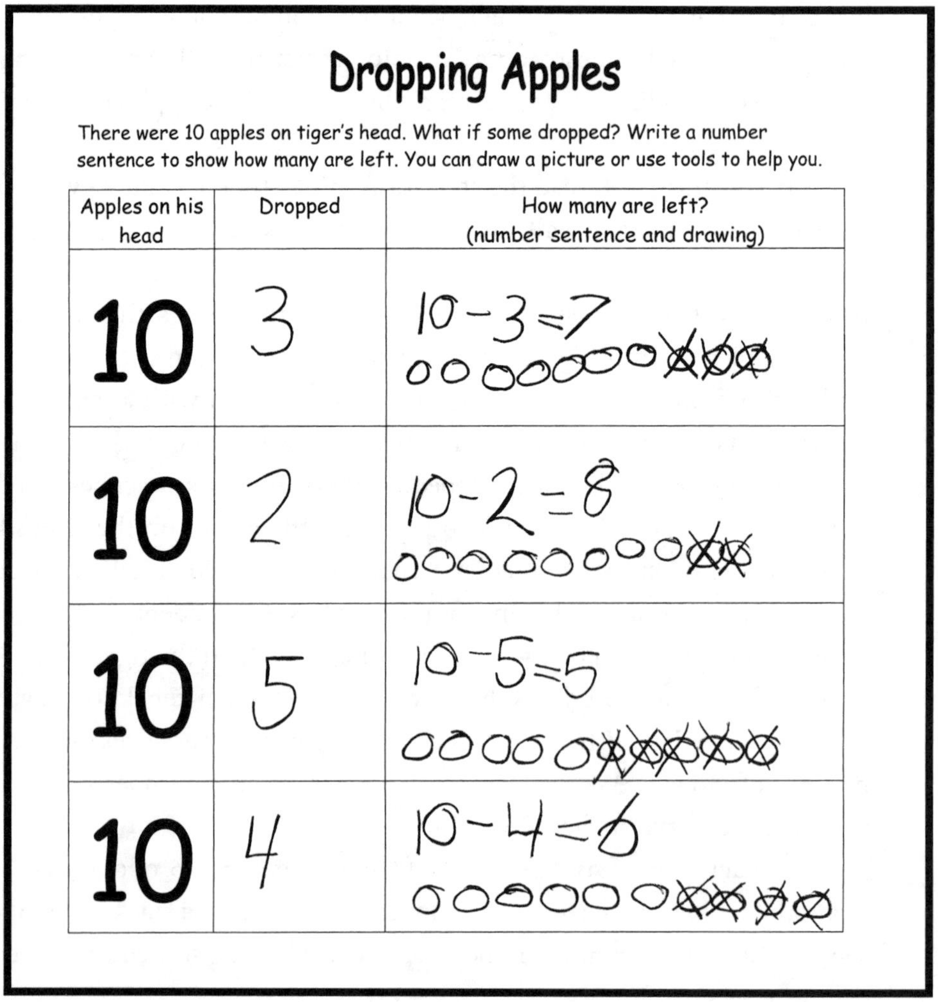

Dropping Apples

There were 10 apples on tiger's head. What if some dropped? Write a number sentence to show how many are left. You can draw a picture or use tools to help you.

Apples on his head	Dropped	How many are left? (number sentence and drawing)
10	3	10 – 3 = 7
10	2	10 – 2 = 8
10	5	10 – 5 = 5
10	4	10 – 4 = 6

Practice for Fluency

How Many More? Players take turns selecting a ten-frame card (see CD) from a facedown stack and tell their partners how many more dots they need to make ten. Students then write subtraction equations to show the facts (i.e., for a card with 7 dots, students write $10 - 7 = 3$).

Towers of 10 This activity is perfect for a math center. All that is needed is a basket of linking cubes and a paper for recording equations. Students create varied towers of 10 using 2 colors of cubes (e.g., 3 red and 7 blue or 4 green and 6 blue). Students then draw a picture of their tower and write the fact family that goes with it.

Behind the Back Provide partners with 10 linking cubes to form a chain. One player puts the chain behind her back and then pulls some cubes off the chain and shows them to her partner. The partner must say how many cubes are still behind his partner's back. The players then check, by counting the cubes that were behind the back, and then start again.

Domino Tens Subtraction Students search for dominoes (see templates on CD) that have a total of 10 dots and write the subtraction equations (e.g., 10 total dots with 4 on one side might be represented by $10 - 4 = 6$). Challenge students to find both related subtraction equations as in Figure 6.7.

Figure 6.7 *This student identifies both subtraction equations represented by the domino.*

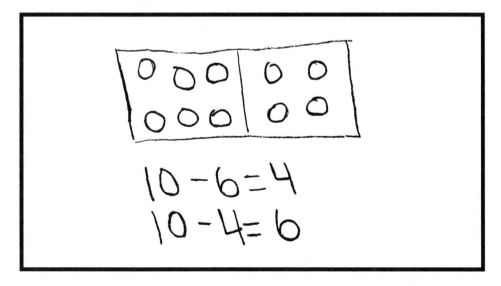

What's Missing? Try the *What's Missing?* activity on the CD to provide a review of both addition and subtraction facts. After students have completed the task by placing the missing values in each number sentence, have them observe the number sentences and write some thoughts about the connection between addition and subtraction facts.

CHAPTER SEVEN

Using 10s

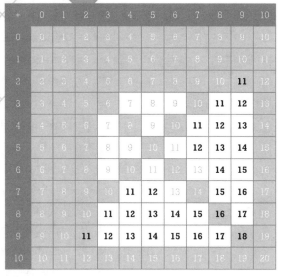

S tudents have now been exposed to the foundation facts (+0, +1, +2, +10, doubles facts, making-ten facts). These facts comprise the bulk of addition math facts. If students are fluent with the foundation facts, they are able to use their knowledge of those facts, along with their understanding of the flexibility of numbers, to find sums for the remaining facts.

KNOWN FACTS   **Using 10s**   TARGETED FACTS   UNKNOWN FACTS

Students access the remaining facts in a variety of ways. One student realizes that $8 + 9 = 17$ because he knows the doubles fact ($8 + 8 = 16$) and 9 is just 1 more than 8, and another student recognizes that $8 + 9 = 17$ by linking it to her understanding of making tens, knowing that $8 + 2 = 10$ and then adding the 7 more to make 17. Both students use their prior knowledge and their understanding of numbers to make sense of the unknown fact. Our explorations and discussions about numbers and properties and students' knowledge of foundation facts give them the power to make sense of unknown facts in a variety of ways. In this chapter and the next, we explore ways that students use knowledge of foundation facts to master the remaining facts. We begin with a focus on using tens.

Using tens is easiest when one addend is either 9 or 8. In these cases, students simply break apart the other addend and add 1 or 2 to make ten. Adding the remaining amount to find the sum is easy, because adding to 10 has already been explored and has proven to be a simple task (i.e., to solve $9 + 6$, students recognize that 10 is 1 more than 9, so they break 6 into $1 + 5$, and add $(9 + 1) + 5$ to find that $10 + 5 = 15$, a much simpler way to think about the fact). Learning to think about numbers flexibly and manipulate them in a way that makes computations easier are skills our students will use throughout their lives as they perform mental math tasks.

Although we know that facts with 8 or 9 as addends are perfect for the making-ten strategy, we recognize that when students have automatic recall of all facts that make ten, they quickly see ways they can break apart one addend to find unknown facts, even if that addend is not an 8 or 9. Students who automatically know $6 + 4 = 10$ will be able to quickly tell you the sum of $6 + 5$. Students who automatically know $7 + 3 = 10$ can tell you why $7 + 4 = 11$.

There are only eleven facts in the making-ten set, and because the order of the addends does not matter, and we do not have to break apart $0 + 10$ because 10 is already an addend, there are only five addend pairs that provide the framework for the using-tens strategy ($9 + 1$, $8 + 2$, $7 + 3$, $6 + 4$, $5 + 5$). Students who know these addend pairs are able to apply their knowledge to a variety of math facts. Repeated practice with this set of facts prior to beginning a focus on using tens is beneficial. If students have automatic recall of these facts, their minds are free to concentrate on ways to break apart addends to create simpler facts. Fluency with facts that make ten and an understanding of the flexibility of numbers provide our students with the thinking skills to find many unknown facts.

Focusing on the Big Ideas

Exploring big ideas about mathematics provides the backdrop for our exploration of using tens. Following are some big ideas.

Working with tens simplifies computations.

When exploring +10 facts, students began to realize that adding any single-digit number to 10 is quite simple. Because of this, if students are able to make tens and then simply add the remaining quantity to that 10, the addition task is simplified. When adding 9 + 3, students make ten by adding 9 + 1 and then add the remaining 2, changing the expression to 10 + 2, a much simpler computation.

Numbers are flexible. They can be broken apart to more easily perform calculations.

Numbers can be composed and decomposed. We can join several smaller sets to form one large set (e.g., 3 and 5 can be joined to make 8) or break one set into smaller sets (e.g., 8 can be broken into sets of 3 and 5). Breaking one addend apart to perform a simpler operation allows us to find sums more easily. When faced with finding the sum of 8 + 7, students might break apart 7 into 2 + 5 and easily find the sum of (8 + 2) + 5, which is simply 10 + 5. The numbers were quickly decomposed and composed to make the calculation more friendly. When breaking numbers apart, a goal is to make ten because of the way it immediately simplifies computations.

Key questions related to the big ideas for using tens are:

How can we simplify this fact?

Do we already know any facts that are close to this?

Can we find a +10 fact that is close? How will that help us? Can we break apart either addend so we can make ten?

How does breaking apart numbers help us find unknown facts?

Our goal is to continually reinforce the big ideas related to math facts as we help students develop addition and subtraction strategies.

Identifying the Fact Set   Within this book, the following facts are designated as *using-ten facts*, but that does not mean it is the only way to think of these facts, nor does it mean that these are the only facts that can be solved by employing using-ten thinking. Math facts with 8 and 9 as addends, that have a sum greater than 10, are a perfect fit for this type of thinking. These facts include: 9 + 2, 9 + 3, 9 + 4, 9 + 5, 9 + 6, 9 + 7, 9 + 8, 9 + 9, 8 + 3, 8 + 4, 8 + 5, 8 + 6, 8 + 7, 8 + 8, 8 + 9. In addition, 7 + 4 and 7 + 5 are included in the fact cards and Fact Checks for this set of facts because thinking of 7 + 3 is a solid approach for simplifying these facts. Many of the other facts with 6 and 7 as addends are not addressed in this chapter in order to keep the fact set smaller and allow for more focused practice and because the remaining unknown facts (e.g., 6 + 5 or 7 + 6) work well with connections to doubles, which will be our next set of facts (see Chapter 8).

Don't worry if students see a fact as a using-ten fact when it is characterized differently within this book. Most of the remaining unknown facts relate to known facts in several ways. Acknowledging and discussing these different ways of thinking about facts expands the thinking of all students within the class, even if they might not have immediately seen that connection.

Understanding Using Tens

Literature Link: *Diary of a Worm*

In *Diary of a Worm* (2003), by Doreen Cronin, a worm's journal tells the good and bad sides about being a worm. Through this story, students explore different combinations of addends that make ten.

Before Reading   Ask students to imagine what it might be like to be a worm. Ask students to turn and share two or three different things that worms do during the day. Tell students that you will be reading a fantasy story about a worm. Remind them that in a fantasy, the characters do things that are not real. Have them listen for all of the things this worm does, and the places he goes, that would not make sense for a real worm.

During Reading   Occasionally ask students if a real worm could do what the worm in the story is doing.

After Reading   Ask students to identify some of the things the worm did and the places he went (e.g., made macaroni necklaces in art class, snuck up on kids at the park, ate his homework at school, went to a school dance, wrote in a diary). This worm liked to socialize with classmates, friends, and family. Give partners a bag of 20 pieces of uncooked macaroni, or gummy worms, to represent 20 worms. Provide partners with a double ten-frame mat (see CD) and paper to record equations. Pose the following problem.

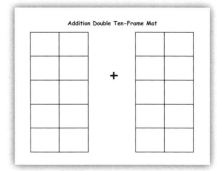

> There are 9 boy worms and 3 girl worms in the class. How many worms are in the class?

Have students place 9 worms on one ten-frame and 3 worms on the other to represent the problem. Record the equation $9 + 3 = \rule{1cm}{0.15mm}$ on the board. Ask partners to solve the problem, observing how they find the sum. Are they counting all of the worms? Are they counting on from 9? Are they using known facts? Are they moving any worms to fill one of the ten-frames?

Have students share their answers and strategies, inserting the answer in the equation on the board. If you observed partners who moved worms to make ten, ask them to share their ideas. If not, share the idea using a think-aloud approach.

I was thinking it might be easier if I just filled in one of the frames. I just moved a worm to this one to make ten. Then it was easy to do 10 + 2.

Tip Using a think-aloud technique allows students to hear your thinking as you adjust and simplify math facts. This technique is extremely helpful as students develop their own thinking related to using known facts to find unknown facts.

Using an overhead projector, document camera, SMART Board, or diagram on chart paper, demonstrate moving a worm from the second frame onto the first frame to fill it. Record the new equation $10 + 2 = 12$. Ask students what they notice about the two equations.

> *Why do they have the same sum?*
> *Are there the same number of worms in all?*
> *Was it easier to find the sum of 9 + 3 or 10 + 2? Why?*

Have students work with partners to represent and solve the following worm problem. Remind them to use their double ten-frame, record the original equation, and then find a simpler equation by making ten.

> There are 8 worms dancing and 4 worms drinking punch at the dance. How many worms are at the dance?

Once they have found solutions, have a brief class discussion to share the two equations. Displaying a double ten-frame on an overhead projector, document camera, or board will help you model their ideas as they explain their thinking. Have students try another worm problem, as in Figure 7.1, as you observe them at work.

> 9 worms ate their math homework and 6 worms ate their reading homework. How many worms ate their homework?

Have a brief class discussion to share the two equations and check for understanding. Then, pose the following worm problem.

> There are 7 worms playing marbles and 9 worms playing hopscotch on the playground. How many worms are on the playground?

Observe as students make tens. They may make ten in different ways. Are they moving 3 worms to complete the frame that started with 7? Are they moving 1 worm to complete the frame that started with 9? After they have explored the problem, discuss the ways students simplified the problem.

How did you make ten?

Which ten-frame did you fill? Is it okay if you didn't fill the same one?

Were your answers the same?

Is there only one way to do it?

Figure 7.1 *This student represents the worm problem on a double ten-frame.*

What was your new number sentence?

Is it okay that some people got 10 + 6 and others got 6 + 10? Will the sum be the same? Why?

Which addend is changed to make ten is not important, although making ten with the largest addend will probably be simpler for most students. What is important is that students recognize that when they move worms to one ten-frame, they are taking them away from the other, so the total number of worms never changes.

Pose another worm problem for additional practice.

> 7 worms drew a picture in art class and 4 painted. How many worms were in art class?

Bring the class together to share their insights about the equations.

Then, tell students that just like the worm, they will be writing in their diaries. Have them write a tip for a friend who can't figure out the answer to 8 + 3. What should they do? How can they make it easier? Remind them that they can use pictures to help them explain their thinking.

Exploring the Facts: Counters In and Out

Visualizing the process of making ten simplifies it for students. Using a single ten-frame and two-color counters is another way for students to visualize this process. Give each student a ten-frame (see CD) and 19 two-color counters. Pull a fact card for students to solve (e.g., 8 + 3). Have students place 8 yellow counters in their ten-frame. Then, have them place 3 red counters outside of the ten-frame. Ask students if it is easy or hard to tell you the sum without counting each counter. Then, have students move 2 red counters into the ten-frame to fill it. How many are left outside the frame (1)? Ask them how many counters in all (10 + 1 = 11). Is it easier to quickly know the sum this time? Did they have to count?

Have students clear their ten-frames and try it again with various using-ten fact cards. Give them opportunities to explore each fact by moving the counters from outside to inside the ten-frame. In Figure 7.2, the student shows how she moved counters onto the ten-frame to create 10 and some more. Encourage students to write the original fact and the using-ten fact.

Tip Even when students are working with partners, it can be helpful to give both students a recording sheet. Working in pairs allows students to share their thinking, but writing allows them to individually process the ideas.

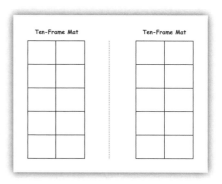

Tip Note that using two-color counters allows students to see the original data even when the counters have been moved inside the ten-frame, as they are still red. Both the original equation and the new equation are visible.

Figure 7.2 *This student began with 9 + 4 and showed how she made ten to shift the fact to the simpler 10 + 3.*

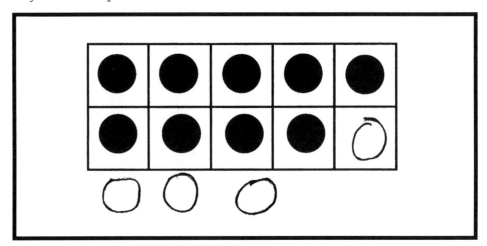

Supporting All Learners

The following classroom activities provide you with additional lesson ideas for the whole class or for small teacher-led groups with students who might need to explore using tens in a different way.

A New Look for Bead Counters   Bead counters were introduced in Chapter 6, allowing students to move beads to observe addends that form 10. As we explore the strategy of using tens, bead counters again offer a simple, hands-on tool for visualizing the strategy. The using-ten strategy focuses on sums beyond 10, so bead counters for this strategy have twenty beads, five beads of four colors as in Figure 7.3. The beads must be able to move along the pipe cleaner so they can be grouped in different ways.

Once students have created their counters, simply show a fact card and have students represent the fact using their bead counter. For example, for 9 + 4, students first move 9 counters to the left side (see Figure 7.4), and then move 4 counters to join them (see Figure 7.5). Students then find the sum by determining the total number of beads in the new group. The colors help students immediately see that the sum is 10 and 3 more.

Figure 7.3 *Bead counters are created with twenty beads of four colors.*

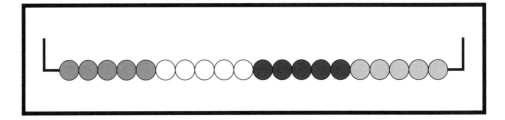

Figure 7.4 *Students move 9 counters to the left. The colored beads allow them to do this without counting.*

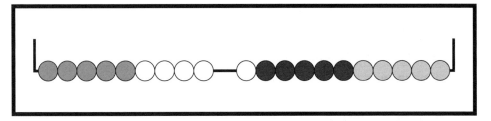

Figure 7.5 *As 4 more beads are moved to the left, students immediately see the "10." 9 + 4 now looks like 10 + 3 on their bead counters.*

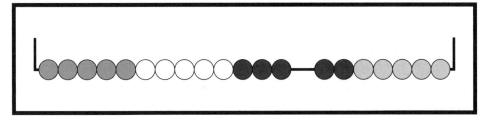

While exploring math facts with bead counters, ask questions to focus students on what they are doing and seeing.

> *When you moved 9 beads to find 9 + 4, did you count the 9 beads? How did you know that it was exactly 9 beads that you moved?*
>
> *How could you find 9 without counting? Did the bead colors help you? How?*
>
> *When you added 4 more to your beads, how did you know the sum was 13?*
>
> *Did you count each bead? Did you see the 10 and 3 more?*
>
> *Is it easier to see the 10 and work from that point or to count every bead? Which way is faster?*

Posing math facts for students to represent using their counters, prompting them to discuss their actions and insights, and having students record the original equations and the new using-ten equations provide students with repeated practice adjusting numbers to simplify computations.

Flip to 10 Students need 19 two-color counters for this hands-on exploration of using tens. Pull a using-ten fact card (see CD) to show to the group. Have students show one addend with red counters and the other addend with yellow counters. Then have them flip some of one color to the other color to make a group of exactly 10 counters of one color (i.e., for 8 + 4, have students show 8 red counters and 4 yellow counters, then flip over some yellow counters until there

Tip Keep some bead counters handy for students who might need additional support, and a hands-on tool, for completing classroom tasks or center activities.

Using Ten Fact Cards—Addition

3	8	4	8
+ 8	+ 3	+ 8	+ 4
5	8	6	8
+ 8	+ 5	+ 8	+ 6
7	8	8	9
+ 8	+ 7	+ 8	+ 8
8	9	9	7
+ 9	+ 9	+ 7	+ 9

are exactly 10 red ones with 2 yellow remaining). Have them tell you the new equation, including the sum, as you record it. Compare the new equation to the original fact card. How are they alike or different? Try it with a few more. It is easier if students make ten with the larger group, flipping some of the counters in the smaller group. Students might be asked to record what they have done by drawing pictures of both equations.

Egg Carton Tens   Each pair of students will need an egg carton and counters to represent eggs. Cut two sections off of each egg carton, leaving ten egg cup sections, and remove the top so it does not open and close as students are working. Pose some egg problems, asking students to show the problems with their counters. Pose the problems one step at a time, observing students as they represent and solve each problem.

> **Yesterday, Farmer Brown gathered 9 eggs from the hen house.**

Have students place 9 counters in their egg carton to represent the eggs, placing 1 counter in each section.

> **Today, Farmer Brown gathered 4 eggs.**

Have students count 4 counters and place them outside the egg carton.

> **How many eggs did he gather altogether?**

Guide students' thinking with questions.

What operation will you use? Why?

Is it easy to add these numbers in your head?

How might you find the answer?

Can you place the 4 counters in the carton? Why?

Can you place some in the carton? How many will fit?

What do you know now? Does knowing there are 10 in the carton help you find the total?

How would we write this addition number sentence?

Have we changed the number of eggs the chicken laid? Why or why not?

Is it easier to add 9 + 4 or 10 + 3? Why?

Tip   Writing math facts horizontally helps students visualize breaking apart or combining addends.

$8 + 5$

$8 + 2 + 3$

$10 + 3$

Pose more egg problems, guiding your students' thinking with questions, observing their work, and listening to their thinking.

Building Automaticity

Students have explored the concept of using tens and are now ready to begin to commit these using-ten facts to memory. The following games and interactive activities give them repeated practice with these facts.

Targeted Practice

Differentiated Math Facts Centers Math centers provide ongoing practice with math facts, as well as an opportunity to differentiate math tasks. Having varied fact card activities at a math facts center allows you to address the needs of various groups of students and ensure that all students are engaged in meaningful practice. While one student selects making-ten fact cards and uses a bead counter to model and then record facts like 8 + 2, another student selects using-ten fact cards and uses bead counters to model and then record facts like 8 + 4.

One center activity might be an interactive game to review doubles for students who still need practice with those facts, and another center task focuses on using tens for students who are ready for practice applying that skill. Familiar activities, modified for the current set of facts, are perfect for centers. Refer to the Additional Resources, included on the CD for each set of facts, for variations of already introduced games to address a new set of math facts.

To promote appropriate behavior at math centers, consider a center reflection sheet on which students indicate at which center they worked, the math they focused on, and their assessment of their effort (see CD).

Double Ten-Frames Students pull a fact card and represent it on a double ten-frame (see CD) by placing counters on each ten-frame to show the two addends. Students record the math fact, then move the counters on the frames to make one 10 and some more. Students record the new addition number sentence and then pull another fact card and begin again.

Tip When focusing on automaticity, consider modifying games by using just the fact cards with 9 as an addend, allowing students some time to build fluency with those facts, and then adding the remaining fact cards in the set.

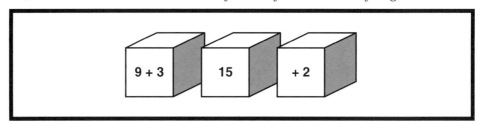

Figure 7.6 *Teacher-made cubes are a fun modification to math fact games.*

Tip Most of the games within this book use number cards, fact cards, or spinners. These game materials are simple and inexpensive to create and very versatile. It is sometimes fun, however, to spice up a game with number cubes. Students enjoy rolling the cubes, which can be store-bought or teacher-created. Many manipulative suppliers sell inexpensive wooden cubes. Teachers can use permanent marker to create game cubes with math facts, numbers, or actions (e.g., +1, +2, or double) as in Figure 7.6. Having students roll the cubes into box tops prevents the cubes from falling to the floor and lessens the noise. Placing cubes in small, clear plastic storage containers (e.g., plastic snack containers) allows students to shake the container with cubes inside, place the container on the desk, and then look through the plastic container to see what was rolled.

Who Has More?   Most of the math games and fact card activities within this book can be easily modified to use with other fact sets. *Who Has More?* (see CD) originally appeared in Chapter Three and was designed to develop the +0 facts. Players each select a fact card, record the equation, and the player with the greater sum wins the round. It is easily modified to practice the using-ten facts by simply substituting the fact card set (see CD for fact cards specifically designed for each fact set). Using familiar game formats keeps students focused on practicing new facts instead of learning the rules to new games.

Condition   *Condition* is a game that offers practice with number concepts while developing automaticity with using-ten facts. Students spread *Condition* cards out on the desk, facedown. The *Condition* cards have statements, or conditions, such as "The sum is an even number or the sum is greater than 14." Fact cards are shuffled and placed facedown in a stack. A player turns over the top fact card and says the sum. He then turns over a *Condition* card. If the sum meets the condition on the card, the player keeps the *Condition* card. If the sum does not meet the condition, it is his opponent's turn and the *Condition* card is returned to its place on the desk. The player with the most condition cards at the end of the game wins.

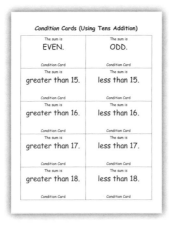

High and Low   *High and Low* can be played with a partner or alone. The using-tens fact cards (see CD) are shuffled and laid in a row facedown. The first card is flipped over and the player tells the sum. Before flipping over the next card, the player predicts whether the sum will be higher or lower than the sum for the previous card. If correct, the player continues on to the next facedown card, predicting whether the sum will be higher or lower than the sum before it. The goal is to successfully predict all of the cards. If a player's prediction is incorrect, all of the cards are picked up, shuffled, and the game starts over. Having a number line (see CD) or bead counter nearby will support students who might need to verify whether a number is greater or less than the number before.

> **Family Math Fact Nights**   Many schools organize Family Math Nights during which parents and children engage in math activities. One goal of Family Math Nights is to educate parents about productive ways to support their children at home. A Math Fact Night is a perfect way to show parents fun ways to help their children gain automaticity with math facts.
>
> A grade level might collaborate to organize a Math Fact Night. Select a few math fact games and gather the materials so parents and students will be able to play them together. Set up game stations with a teacher or adult volunteer at each station. Have a rotation signal (a bell or announcement) so parents and children know when to rotate to the next station. Have enough materials so parents can take home the supplies needed to play the games. The goal is for parents to learn several games that can be easily played at home.

Monitoring Progress

Observing Fact Checks   Observing students as they take Fact Checks is insightful. Which facts are automatic? Which facts slow them down? Which facts bring them to a complete stop? Many teachers carry a clipboard during Fact Checks and discretely jot down observations that might help them identify students who need additional support. The purpose of Fact Checks is to help us identify students' needs. Those needs can be identified by the facts students miss or students' behavior as they attempt the facts.

Connecting to Subtraction

Literature Link: Revisiting *Diary of a Worm*

Reread *Diary of a Worm* (Cronin 2003) or remind students of the events in the story. Pose this story-related problem for students to solve.

> 13 worms went to the school dance. 9 of them did the hokey-pokey. How many did not do the hokey-pokey?

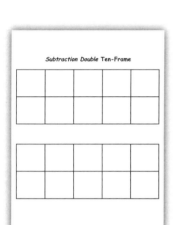

Subtraction Double Ten-Frame

Provide a subtraction double ten-frame (see CD) and 19 counters to pairs of students. Have students work together to solve the problem, suggesting that the double ten-frame might be a tool to help them. Observe students as they explore the problem. When they have found the answer, discuss their answer and how they arrived at it. Did some students use the double ten-frame as in Figure 7.7? Modeling this on an overhead projector, document camera, or SMART Board will help it make more sense to students who did not approach the problem in this way.

Did some students make an easier 10 fact by subtracting 10 from 13 to get 3 and then, because they took 1 too many away (10 rather than the 9 stated in the problem), adding 1 back to get the answer 4? This thinking illustrates an alternate method for subtracting 8 or 9, which is to subtract 10 and then add the 2 or 1 more.

Did some students use the known addition fact, knowing that the difference between 13 and 9 is 4 because 9 + 4 = 13? Highlight the different ways they solved the subtraction problem. Ask students which ways to subtract these numbers seemed easiest to them. Although some students easily see one method, others may struggle to see it. The goal is for all students to master the facts in a way that makes sense to them. Ultimately, mastering the using-ten addition facts provides the quickest route to mastery of the using-ten subtraction facts.

Have students practice their subtraction by posing more worm problems.

> The worms made 14 macaroni necklaces. They ate 8 of them. How many were left?

> There were 15 girls playing in the park. 9 of them screamed when they saw the worm. How many did not scream?

Figure 7.7 *This student represents the problem in three steps using a double ten-frame.*

1. This student first represents the 13 worms with counters on the double ten-frame.

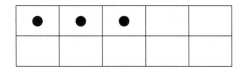

2. The student then removes counters for the 9 worms that did the hokey-pokey. The easiest way to remove 9 would be to take all but 1 counter from the filled ten-frame.

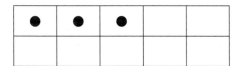

3. The student reorganizes the ten-frames by moving the 1 remaining counter to the other frame and clearly sees the 4 remaining worms that did not do the hokey-pokey.

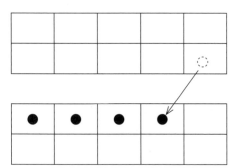

> The worm did 12 pages of homework. He ate 8 of them. How many did he have left?

Practice for Fluency

Difference Maker   For *Difference Maker*, students take turns pulling cards from a shuffled deck of using-ten fact cards (see CD) and record their fact with the difference on the *Difference Maker* recording sheet (see CD). The player with the greatest difference for the round circles it and wins the round. The player who wins the most rounds wins the game. The game board has space for two players but more than two players could play at the same time.

Take Away   In *Take Away*, students play with partners or groups and try to be the first player to take away all of the cards in front of them. Each player begins with a set of ten *Take Away* cards (see CD). These cards are placed faceup in a row in front of players. Each player also has a set of using-ten fact cards. Players shuffle the fact cards and take turns picking one fact card. If they see the difference in their row of *Take Away* cards, they take the card away (remove it or turn it over). The first player to take away all ten cards is the winner.

Mystery Word Problems   Each student picks a using-ten subtraction fact card from a class deck and writes her favorite thing on the back (e.g., ice cream cone, puppies, basketball, stickers). Put all of the fact cards in a bag. Students work with a partner and pick one at random, then write a word problem using the fact and the "favorite thing." Partners should solve their problem and draw a picture to show how they solved it. Have partners share their word problems and solutions with the class, or challenge the class to solve the student-written problems.

Triangle Fact Cards   Triangle Fact Cards (see CD), introduced in Chapter Four, are a great way to provide practice with both addition and subtraction facts. Think *part-part-whole*. The whole is the circled number. Have students work with partners, covering one corner of the card. Can their partner tell the missing part? If both parts are showing, can their partner tell the whole?

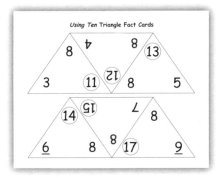

CHAPTER EIGHT

Using Doubles

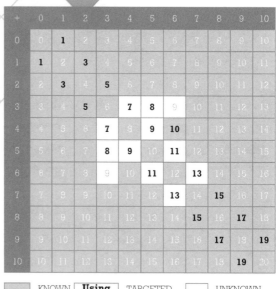

+	0	1	2	3	4	5	6	7	8	9	10
0	0	1	2	3	4	5	6	7	8	9	10
1	1	2	3	4	5	6	7	8	9	10	11
2	2	3	4	5	6	7	8	9	10	11	12
3	3	4	5	6	7	8	9	10	11	12	13
4	4	5	6	7	8	9	10	11	12	13	14
5	5	6	7	8	9	10	11	12	13	14	15
6	6	7	8	9	10	11	12	13	14	15	16
7	7	8	9	10	11	12	13	14	15	16	17
8	8	9	10	11	12	13	14	15	16	17	18
9	9	10	11	12	13	14	15	16	17	18	19
10	10	11	12	13	14	15	16	17	18	19	20

KNOWN FACTS | **Using Doubles** | TARGETED FACTS | UNKNOWN FACTS

Our number of unknown math facts has been reduced to quite a small group. Our focus now is on helping our students use their known facts to find these unknown facts. In the previous chapter, we focused on using knowledge of facts with a sum of 10 to find near-ten facts. We extended our students' understanding of numbers by helping them decompose and compose numbers to make simpler facts, facts with 10 and some more, and then we provided practice with these using-ten facts to allow students to commit them to memory. To expand students'

math fact repertoire, we capitalize on their knowledge of doubles facts to explore doubles plus one more. The only unknown facts in the doubles-plus-one fact set are: 3 + 4, 4 + 5, 5 + 6, and 6 + 7 and their inverses. We also include 3 + 5 in this fact set as a doubles-plus-two fact. It is likely that most students will already know the answer to this fact by employing another strategy (e.g., counting on 3 or using tens), but relating it to doubles is also a reasonable way to find this sum.

As we explore this final fact set, we recognize that students may choose different strategies when exploring unknown facts. Our chart of known facts becomes a bit messy, as some of the remaining facts can be found by employing several different strategies. Does 6 + 5 belong with using tens because 6 + 4 = 10 and it is just 1 more, or does 6 + 5 belong with near doubles because 5 + 5 = 10 and it is just 1 more? Both ways of thinking simplify the fact.

Our goal is to help our students better understand numbers and properties so that they are able to use their existing knowledge to make sense of unknown facts. Explorations and discussions about numbers, patterns, and properties expand students' thinking and provide them with a rich strategy base for math fact mastery. They may not all approach an unknown math fact using the same strategy, but approaching it in the same way is not important—our goal is for them to approach it in a way that makes sense.

Focusing on the Big Ideas

Exploring big ideas about mathematics provides the backdrop for our exploration of near-doubles facts. Some big ideas follow.

Doubling is the process of joining two groups of the same quantity.

Doubling is joining two *like* groups. Both parts that make up the whole are equal quantities.

Halving is the opposite of doubling.

Separating a set into two equal groups results in halves. By halving a set, we can find the quantity for the two equal parts that make the whole. Separating half from a set will result in a difference that is the same as the amount that was separated (i.e., in 12 − 6 = 6, 6 was separated from the set and 6 remains in the set).

There are many strategies to simplify math facts.

Math facts can be thought of in multiple ways. The stronger our understanding of numbers, the more ways we can approach math facts. The strategies we have discussed throughout this book can be applied to a variety of math facts. One student might think of 9 + 2 as counting on 2, and another makes ten to solve the new equation 10 + 1.

Key questions related to the big ideas for near-doubles facts are:

How can we simplify this fact?

Do we already know any facts that are close to this?

Can we find a doubles fact that is close? How might that help us?

Is that the only way to simplify this fact? How else might you think about the fact?

Our goal is to continually reinforce the big ideas related to math facts as we help students develop addition and subtraction strategies.

Understanding Using Doubles

Literature Link: *Fish Eyes*

Fish Eyes, by Lois Ehlert (1990), is filled with illustrations of fish in many different shapes and sizes. Each page shows a different quantity of striped or skinny or flashy or flipping fish, setting the context for fishy problems in which the doubles-plus-one strategy is explored.

Before Reading   Tell students that you will be reading a story about fish and to turn and tell a partner some words that might describe a fish. Are fish fast or slippery or spotted? Make a fish word web on the board, recording students' descriptive words about fish.

During Reading   While reading, have students identify the number of fish and the word or words that are used to describe the fish. Check the class web to see if the descriptive word appears on your list.

After Reading   Have students recall the different numbers and types of fish. If students have trouble, look through the book to find different examples. After identifying a few examples pose the following problem.

> There were 4 striped fish and 5 spotted fish. How many fish were there altogether?

Have students work with partners to solve the problem. Observe them as they work. Did they draw and count the fish? Did they use any of their previous fact knowledge? If any student employs a using-doubles approach, have them share their thinking with the class. If not, try a think-aloud technique in which you share using-doubles thinking.

> *This fact looks a lot like 4 + 4. Only one number is different, it's a 5 instead of 4. It seems like it would be just 1 more than 4 + 4. 4 + 4 = 8, so I think 4 + 5 = 9.*

Ask students if your thinking makes sense. Is your answer the same as theirs? You have exposed them to using-doubles thinking. Pose more problems and ask students to find a double that looks close to the math fact for each problem. Can they do some using-doubles thinking to solve these problems?

> There were 3 smiling fish and 4 striped fish. How many fish were there altogether?

> There were 5 spotted fish and 6 fantail fish. How many fish were there altogether?

> There were 6 fantail fish and 7 flipping fish. How many fish were there altogether?

Have students share their thinking about how they solved each problem. Was there an easy way to do the computations? Did knowing doubles simplify these problems? The student in Figure 8.1 shares how she solved a problem with the number sentence $3 + 4 = 7$.

Work with a small group if you find some students who need additional support. Provide a review of doubles facts or opportunities to visualize the concept using manipulatives, or goldfish crackers, to create two rows of fish, with one row being just 1 more than the other.

As you work with a small group, have others work with partners to practice their using-doubles thinking. List the different numbers and types of fish in order (this chart can be prepared before the class) and have students choose two types of fish that are one number apart and build number sentences to

Figure 8.1 *This student recognized 3 + 4 as near the doubles fact 3 + 3 and explains how using doubles helped her find the sum.*

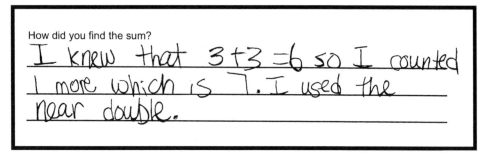

> How did you find the sum?
>
> I knew that 3+3=6 so I counted 1 more which is 7. I used the near double.

show the sum. Have them practice adding the two numbers together by doubling the smaller number and adding 1 more.

Exploring the Facts: Doubles and One More

Prior to exploring using doubles to find unknown facts, students should have quick recall of doubles facts. Reviewing doubles facts through whole-class or partner fact card reviews, doubles tasks at a math center, and revisiting doubles games will set the stage for an easy transition to using doubles. Revisit Chapter Five for a variety of doubles activities.

Once students have reviewed doubles facts, begin a whole-class fact card practice with the facts, using a think-pair-share technique. As you show a doubles fact card, cue students to think, pair, and share the sums.

1. *Think:* Think about the sum. Don't raise your hand. Don't say the answer.

2. *Pair:* Turn and tell your partner the sum.

3. *Share:* Raise your hand and share the sum with the class.

Begin with doubles facts, but tell students you will be adding some new fact cards. Show students 4 + 4 and have them think-pair-share. Then show 4 + 5. As students share their ideas, draw a simple diagram on the board of a row of 4 dots and a row of 5 dots right below them. Record *4 + 4 + 1*. Ask students some questions to prompt their thinking:

How is this like doubles? How is it different?

Would knowing 4 + 4 help you find 4 + 5? How?

Is 4 + 5 the same as 4 + 4 plus 1 more (4 + 4 + 1)? Explain.

Tip It is easier for most students to double the smaller number and then add 1 to find the sum. Doubling the larger number and subtracting 1 will also result in the correct sum but can be more difficult for some students to understand.

Show students the 5 + 5 fact card, followed by the 5 + 6 fact card. Again, ask students to turn and tell a partner how the two fact cards are alike and how they are different. Draw a diagram and record 5 + 5 + 1.

Show students the 6 + 6 fact card, followed by the 6 + 7 fact card. Again, ask students to turn and tell a partner how the two fact cards are alike and how they are different. Draw a diagram and record 6 + 6 + 1.

For the initial practice, begin with the doubles fact and then show the doubles-plus-one fact. Posing fact cards with the same initial number (e.g., 7 + 7, 7 + 8) helps students easily see the similarities in the two fact cards and allows them to double the first (lower) addend. Once students gain confidence with doubles-plus-one thinking, pose some fact cards with the addends reversed (e.g., 7 + 7, 8 + 7). Discuss how the facts are alike and different. Remind students that the order of the addends does not matter. Doubling the lower one and adding 1 will allow them to find the double-plus-one sum.

Give doubles-plus-one fact cards to partners and have them work together to select a card and find the sum. Have partners make a list of doubles-plus-one facts. Once students have had some time to explore the facts, have them work with partners to share a tip for someone just learning these facts. The student in Figure 8.2, using the example 4 + 5, explains how to use 4 + 4 to find the sum.

Supporting All Learners

The following classroom activities provide you with additional lesson ideas for the whole class or for small teacher-led groups with students who might need to explore near-doubles facts in a different way.

Figure 8.2 *Using his understanding of a doubles fact allows this student to find the sum of a near double.*

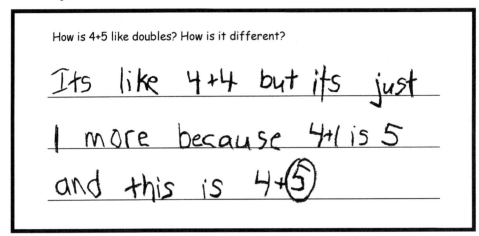

How is 4+5 like doubles? How is it different?

Its like 4+4 but its just 1 more because 4+1 is 5 and this is 4+⑤

Near-Doubles Trains   Students will need 10 linking cubes of two different colors (e.g., 10 green and 10 blue), a 1–9 spinner, and a *Near-Doubles Trains* recording sheet (see CD). Students spin the spinner to determine how many cubes of one color should be linked to make a train. They then make a second train, of a different color, using that number of cubes plus 1 more. Students link the two trains together and determine how many cubes there are in all as in Figure 8.3. Students record what they have done by coloring the train recording sheet and writing the near-doubles equation. Then, they take apart the train and spin again to create a new near-doubles train.

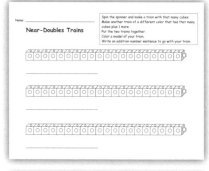

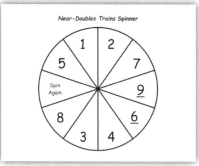

Revisit *Fish Eyes*   Revisit *Fish Eyes* by Lois Ehlert, this time posing doubles-plus-one problems and having students act out the problems using goldfish crackers or manipulatives. Have students line the two sets of goldfish in two rows, like goldfish swimming, to show the doubles plus one more. Record number sentences to represent each math fact (e.g., *4 + 5* and *4 + 4 + 1*). After doing a few, have students predict the sum before lining up the goldfish. Are they beginning to use their understanding of doubles to find the new sum?

Figure 8.3 *This student explores near-doubles facts by creating trains with linking cubes.*

Sorting Doubles Fact Cards   Mix a set of doubles fact cards and near-doubles fact cards (see CD). Have students sort the cards into two categories: doubles and near doubles. Have them match each doubles fact with a near-doubles partner (e.g., 5 + 5 might be matched with 5 + 6 or 6 + 5) and tell the sums of the math facts. Emphasize the connection between the doubles and near doubles and how knowing the doubles fact allows students to quickly find the near-doubles fact. Keep in mind that students might match the near-facts a little differently because 6 + 5 might be thought of as a near-double of 5 + 5 or 6 + 6.

> **Doubles Plus Two**   Many students see 3 + 5 as a doubles-plus-two fact. Doubles plus two is a way to think of many facts like 6 + 8 or 4 + 6 or 5 + 7; however, those facts have been discussed during other strategy sets. Discussing doubles plus two is a nice way to provide a strategy for 3 + 5 and to spark insights about other facts that might be double plus two more. Remember the impact of hands-on explorations, pulling out those linking cubes to create doubles-plus-two chains.

Building Automaticity

It is time to begin practice sessions so students have repeated exposure to the near-doubles facts. It is through these practice tasks that students begin to commit the facts to memory.

Targeted Practice

Trimming Down Fact Card Decks   Fact cards can be used to review one set of facts (e.g., only the near-doubles facts) or might be used to review previously learned facts. As students become more skilled, removing some of the facts that have already been mastered (e.g., +0, +1, +2, +10) reduces the quantity of cards and provides more repetition of the targeted facts.

Home Practice with Math Facts Games   Games can be a motivating home assignment. Parents are often willing but unsure how to help their children at home. Math fact games provide parents with specific activities that support their children's math skills and provide for fun family time. Before sending games home, be sure that your students have had an opportunity to play the game in school and clearly understand how the game is played. Older siblings might also be enlisted for home practice when parents are not avail-

Tip   Fact card activities often feel more like games than math practice tasks, so students choose these activities during indoor recess, before the morning bell, or when they have completed class assignments. Every exposure to the facts moves students a step closer to automatic recall.

able. See the CD for a parent letter inviting parents to play math fact games with their children. The letter includes some quick ideas for at-home games. Use this letter as a template to design your own parent letter.

Spin and Double It   In *Spin and Double It*, students work with partners to explore doubles facts. One partner spins the 3–9 spinner (see CD) to find the starting number. The other partner spins the doubles wheel (see CD) to find out if they will be finding the double or double plus one. Partners then work together to write the number sentences.

Match 'Em Up   In *Match 'Em Up*, partners spread out near-doubles math fact cards and double-plus-one math fact cards (see CD). For example, a player might match 3 + 4 to 3 + 3 + 1. Students match the cards and record their matches on the *Match 'Em Up* recording sheet (see CD).

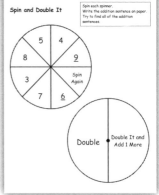

Almost Doubles   In *Almost Doubles*, students take turns spinning the near-doubles spinner, stating the sum, and recording it in the appropriate section of their *Almost Doubles* recording sheet (see CD), which is simply an addition

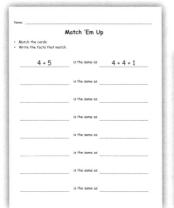

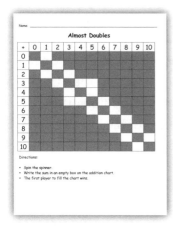

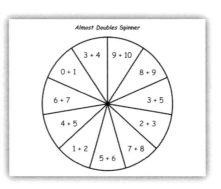

chart with all sections shaded except the sections to record near-doubles facts. Remind students that 2 + 3 and 3 + 2 have the same sum, so can be recorded in either of the two places where those addends intersect on the chart. If a player spins a sum that has already been recorded in both places on the chart, he loses that turn. The first player to complete his chart by filling in all of the blank spaces is the winner.

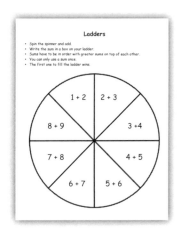

Ladders   *Ladders* provides practice with near-doubles facts and challenges students to order numbers from least to greatest. To play *Ladders*, two students take turns spinning a near-doubles spinner and recording the sum on a vertical number line (see CD). The sums must be recorded in order from least (bottom) to greatest (top) as in Figure 8.4. If a student spins a sum and does not have a place to put it on his ladder, he loses his turn. The first player to complete his ladder is the winner.

Monitoring Progress

Individual Conferencing   As students work to master their using-doubles facts, taking the time to confer with individual students allows you to assess their progress and focus them on specific goals. As the students in your class are engaged in practice tasks or visiting math centers, invite individual students to meet with you to review their most recent Fact Check. Examine blank or incorrect math facts. Ask students which facts are difficult for them to remember. Provide tips and reminders to help students master those facts. Record a few unknown facts on index cards and give the cards to the student to take home to practice. Praise each student for the facts she does know and encourage each student to continue reviewing the unknown facts.

Gathering Data Through Observations   Frequently move through the room observing partners as they explore using-doubles facts. Listening to their discussions provides great insight into their understanding and mastery. Jotting down observations allows you to plan for future interventions, lesson adjustments, or task modifications.

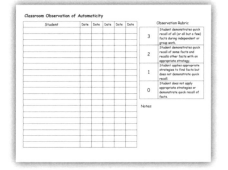

As you observe students, think about their progress toward automaticity. Are they immediately recalling all of the facts? Are they immediately recalling some facts, but using appropriate strategies to find others? Are you failing to see evidence of immediate recall or appropriate strategies? See the CD for a classroom observation form that might help you document your observations.

Figure 8.4 *Anna spins 4 + 5 but cannot place the sum on her ladder because she does not have a space for it between the 7 and 11. She loses this turn.*

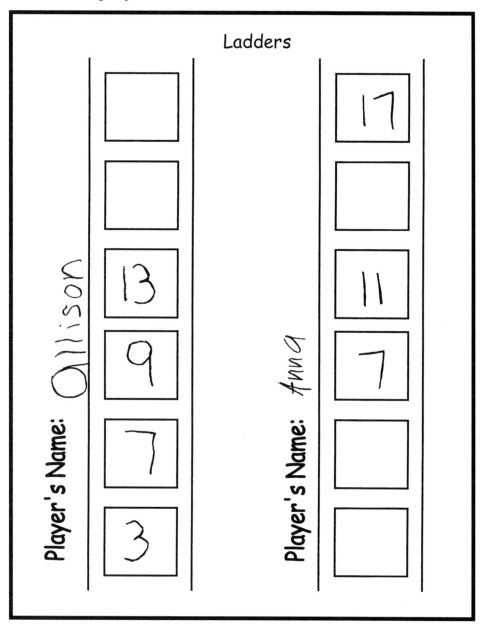

Connecting to Subtraction

Exploring About Half

When we explored doubles in addition, we made connections to the concept of halves in subtraction. The two addends in a doubles number sentence each represent half of the sum, because the addends are always the same quantity. Remembering the concept of halves simplifies finding the difference for doubles subtraction.

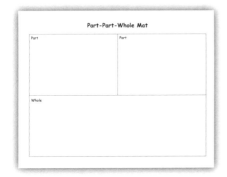

When exploring near-doubles, the addends are about half. Support students in developing this number sense by flashing a near-doubles sum (e.g., 13) and asking students to identify about half (i.e., 6 or 7 would make sense). Capitalize on a couple minutes here or there throughout the day to practice finding about half. Recognizing about half helps students assess the reasonableness of their math fact computations.

Revisiting *Fish Eyes* to Solve Subtraction Problems

Pose some subtraction problems related to the fish that appear in *Fish Eyes* to challenge students to explore using-doubles in subtraction. Provide students with 19 goldfish crackers, or manipulatives, a part-part-whole chart (see CD), and some paper for recording number sentences. Pose the following problem for students to investigate with a partner.

> There were 11 fish. 5 were spotted. How many were not spotted?

Have students use their manipulatives to represent the problem, selecting 11 goldfish and placing them in the *whole* section of their chart. Students then move the part they know (5 spotted fish) to one of the *part* sections. How many are left? Students move the remaining fish to the other *part* section and check their answers. Students then write a subtraction number sentence to show the differences (11 − 5 = 6). Have students look at the *parts* sections and describe what they see.

Are the number of fish in the two groups almost the same?

If you lined up each group to compare them, what is the difference between the two groups?

Have students work with partners to explore more fish problems, encouraging them to predict the answers before using their manipulatives to solve the problem. Try problems like these:

> There were 17 fish. 8 were skinny. How many were not skinny?

> There were 7 fish. 4 were striped. How many were not striped?

> There were 15 fish. 7 were flipping. How many were not flipping?

> There were 9 fish. 5 were spotted. How many were not spotted?

17 − 8 = 9	9 + 8 = 17
7 − 4 = 3	3 + 4 = 7
15 − 7 = 8	8 + 7 = 15
9 − 5 = 4	4 + 5 = 9

Figure 8.5 *Recording equations side by side helps students identify the connection between them.*

Have students share some of their subtraction number sentences as you record them on the board. Ask them to talk with partners to share any observations about the equations. Do the numbers look familiar? Record each addition equation next to the subtraction equation as in Figure 8.5. Have students share their insights.

Practicing for Fluency

Missing Numbers *Missing Numbers* contains a series of near-doubles subtraction equations with missing values. Players take turns flipping over a 1–9 number card (see CD) and recording the number in one of the blanks on their *Missing Numbers* recording sheet (see CD). The player reads the fact out loud and then places the number back in the deck and reshuffles. If a number can't be used, that player loses his turn. The first player to fill all of the missing values is the winner.

Two versions of the game worksheet appear on the CD. One version has missing values for the differences, and the other is a more complex version with the blanks appearing in different places in the equations. Although the simpler version may be perfect for some of your students, the challenge of the more complex version will benefit others.

Tip Automatic recall of addition facts is the most efficient way for students to gain fluency with related subtraction facts.

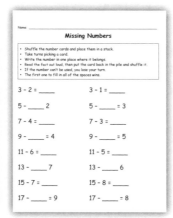

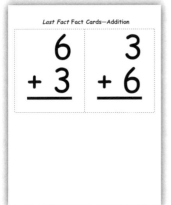

Fact Family Chains *Fact Family Chains* provides practice with addition and subtraction near-double facts. Partners require nine linking cubes each of two different colors and 2–8 cards (see CD). Players pick a card at random and use linking cubes of one color to create a chain with that number of cubes. Players then create a second chain of a different color that is 1 cube longer than the first. For example, if Jill picks a 4, she creates a chain with 4 blue cubes and then a red chain with 5 cubes, 1 more than on the blue chain. Students then connect the two chains and work together to write the four fact family equations to represent the near-doubles fact (e.g., $4 + 5 = 9$; $5 + 4 = 9$; $9 - 5 = 4$; $9 - 4 = 5$).

One Lonely Fact

Our students have now explored foundation facts (+1, +2, +0, +10, doubles, making ten) and have identified ways to use their knowledge of tens and doubles to find the sums of many unknown facts. The only fact that has not been addressed by one of our strategies is $3 + 6$. The greater our students' understanding of numbers, the more likely this fact will be understood by its connection to other known facts. Introduce students to this *one lonely fact* and ask them how they will remember the fact.

Students might think of $3 + 6$ as doubles plus 3 more. Or they might think of it as almost 10 because $4 + 6$ would be 10 and it is just 1 less. Some students might simply begin with 6 and count on 3 more to find the sum. After discussing possible strategies for this fact, have students share their ideas about finding the sum on the *One Lonely Fact* recording sheet (see CD). To ensure that students have practice opportunities with this fact, include the $3 + 6$ fact cards (see CD) with your center activities or practice tasks.

Retaining Math Facts

Even after students have explored and practiced each set of math facts, they benefit from cumulative practice activities to review and retain the facts. Place math fact games in centers or schedule a fact review several times a week. Try the following practice tasks to target problematic fact sets or simply to provide an ongoing review of all facts.

Facts Card Sorting

Students work in teams of two to four to find answers to math facts and then sort the facts into categories based on the sums. You might provide them with fact cards for using tens, using doubles, and the one lonely fact. Some sorting possibilities are:

- sums that are even numbers or odd numbers

- sums less than 10; sums 11 or more

- sums that are two-digit or one-digit numbers

Fact Card Face-Off

Fact Card Face-Off is played like the traditional card game of *War*. Fact cards are shuffled and dealt to two players. Select fact cards that target specific student needs or that focus on a current strategy. Each player pulls a fact card from her stack and states the sum. The player with the greater sum is the winner and gets to keep both fact cards. Players then each pull another card from the top of their decks and continue. (An addition chart may be kept facedown to check any questionable answers.) Play continues until one player has all of the cards. This game can be modified by using subtraction fact cards.

Math Checkers

This variation of the traditional game of *Checkers* requires students to solve a math fact as they land on it. The *Math Checkers* board on the CD is filled with near-doubles facts, as well as the one fact (3 + 6) that was not addressed as a part of a strategy set. This game can quickly become a targeted review of any set of unknown facts by simply changing the facts on the board.

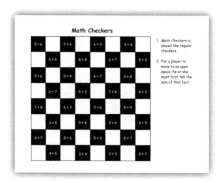

Scrambled Eggs

Use magic marker to write a number from 4–9 in the bottom of each cup section of an egg carton. You will have to write each number in two different cups. Place two small cubes in the egg carton, close the lid, and have students gently shake the carton. When they open the carton, they must find the sum of the two numbers on which the chips or blocks have settled. Students can play with a partner or can play in teams, keeping score by recording a tally mark for each time their sum was greater than their opponent's sum. The player, or team, with the most tallies wins the game.

Automatic Recall of Facts

Our goal is for our students to have automatic recall of math facts. We don't want them to have to think about the facts. We want them to simply know the sums and differences. To get there, however, our students require many opportunities to explore the facts, to discuss and develop their understanding of numbers and properties, and to engage in repeated practice. Although we recognize the importance of automatic recall, asking students to simply memorize sets of facts is not the answer. Automatic recall comes from repeated opportunities to explore and interact with math facts. It comes from following a progression of tasks that allow students to gain expertise in chunks and then build on their existing knowledge to continually expand their repertoire of facts. When we follow this progression, our students know more than their math facts—they understand numbers and are ready to begin the challenges of more complex computations.

Conclusion

Automaticity with basic math facts provides a solid foundation that supports students as they are continually challenged by the increasing complexity of math skills. But our goals in teaching math facts are much broader than simply providing students with automatic recall of sets of facts. Through explorations with patterns, properties, operations, and number concepts, we focus on building a greater understanding of numbers. To do this, we must rethink the teaching of math facts to include the following principles.

1. The focus of math fact instruction is on understanding numbers and operations. The exploration of patterns and properties helps students make sense of math facts. Big ideas about numbers form the backdrop for math facts instruction.

2. Exploring the meanings of operations is essential before any memorization efforts begin. Connecting math facts to real-world experiences and providing investigations to explore math facts attaches meaning to the facts.

3. A teaching sequence that builds on previously learned facts demonstrates the interconnectedness of the facts and supports student learning. Students are able to connect each new set of facts to previous knowledge.

4. Talk and writing during the exploration and practice of math facts helps students process ideas and make sense of math facts. Verbalizing observations, making conjectures, justifying solutions, and explaining their thought processes push students to think deeply about numbers.

5. Automaticity takes time. Frequent, varied, and repeated practice moves students toward automaticity. Math facts are not learned through single lessons, but through a series of lessons and practice tasks that are woven together to provide a strong program.

6. Although fluency is a goal, the importance of speed should be minimized to build students' confidence and skills simultaneously. Fluency should be assessed in multiple ways including teacher observation, individual conferences, and Fact Checks.

7. Some students require additional support through small-group or individualized interventions with more and different types of math

fact explorations. Providing additional opportunities for some students to visualize and discuss math facts will support their path toward mastery.

8. Mastery of math facts is only one aspect of mathematical competency. Regardless of where students might be in their pursuit of automaticity, it is important to continue to expose them to a wide range of math skills.

9. The expectations and support of teachers can increase or decrease the anxiety felt by students as they work to master basic facts. Celebration of successes, provision of needed support, connections to prior knowledge, and careful selection of targeted practice activities afford all students a less stressful experience.

Our goal is to build strong mathematicians. Mastery of math facts is an important step toward that goal. If math fact instruction is thoughtful and strategic, it results in more than a student's ability to quickly recall a fact; it cultivates reflective students who have a greater understanding of numbers and a flexibility of thinking that allows them to understand connections between mathematical ideas. It develops the skills and attitudes that allow students to tackle the future challenges of mathematics.

References

Professional References

Carpenter, T. P., E. Fennema, M. L. Franke, L. Levi, and S. B. Empson. 1999. *Children's Mathematics: Cognitively Guided Instruction.* Portsmouth, NH: Heinemann.

Fosnot, C. T., and M. Dolk. 2001. *Young Mathematicians at Work: Constructing Number Sense, Addition, and Subtraction.* Portsmouth, NH: Heinemann.

Fuson, K. C. 2003. "Developing Mathematical Power in Whole Number Operations." In *A Research Companion to Principles and Standards for School Mathematics.* Reston, VA: National Council of Teachers of Mathematics.

Gravemeijer, K., and F. van Galen. 2003. "Facts and Algorithms as Products of Students' Own Mathematical Activity." In *A Research Companion to Principles and Standards for School Mathematics.* Reston, VA: National Council of Teachers of Mathematics.

Marzano, R. J., D. Pickering, and J. E. Pollock. 2001. *Classroom Instruction That Works: Research-Based Strategies for Increasing Student Achievement.* Alexandria, VA: Association for Supervision and Curriculum Development.

National Council of Teachers of Mathematics. 2000. *Principles and Standards for School Mathematics.* Reston, VA: National Council of Teachers of Mathematics.

National Governors Association Center for Best Practices and Council of Chief State School Officers. 2010. *Common Core State Standards for Mathematics.* Available at: www.corestandards.org/assets/CCSSI_Math%20Standards .pdf. Accessed on July 28, 2010.

National Mathematics Advisory Panel. 2008. *Foundations for Success: The Final Report of the National Mathematics Advisory Panel.* Washington, D.C.: U.S. Department of Education.

Van de Walle, J. 2004. *Elementary and Middle School Mathematics, Teaching Developmentally,* 5th ed. New York: Pearson Education.

Wiggins, G., and J. McTighe. 1998. *Understanding by Design.* Alexandria, VA: Association for Supervision and Curriculum Development.

Children's Literature

Baker, A. 1994. *Gray Rabbit's 1, 2, 3.* Boston: Kingfisher.

Carle, E. 1972. *Rooster's Off to See the World.* New York: Aladdin Paperbacks.

Cronin, D. 2003. *Diary of a Worm.* New York: Scholastic.

Ehlert, L. 1990. *Fish Eyes.* New York: Harcourt.

Meddaugh, S. 1996. *Martha Blah Blah*. New York: Houghton Mifflin Harcourt.

Murphy, S. 1997. *Elevator Magic*. New York: HarperCollins.

———. 1998. *Animals on Board*. New York: HarperCollins.

———. 2003. *Double the Ducks*. New York: HarperCollins.

Numeroff, L. 1985. *If You Give a Mouse a Cookie*. New York: HarperCollins Children's Books.

Sierra, J. 1997. *Counting Crocodiles*. New York: Harcourt.

Seuss, Dr. writing as Theo LeSieg. 1961. *Ten Apples up on Top!* New York: Random House.

Walsh, E. Stoll. 1991. *Mouse Count*. New York: Harcourt.

Ward, N. 1998. *Don't Eat the Teacher!* New York: Scholastic.

Wise, W. 1993. *Ten Sly Piranhas*. New York: Scholastic.

Professional Learning Communities Study Guide

Learning is inherently social. As teachers, it is easy to feel isolated. It becomes especially important that we find opportunities to talk with colleagues and reflect on our teaching practices. Through professional learning communities, we hear new ideas, consider new techniques, clarify our thinking, and ultimately enhance our teaching. It is through conversations with colleagues that we grow as teachers. Teacher study groups value the experience and knowledge of teachers. They provide a forum for rich discussions about teaching and learning. They motivate us to try new approaches and assess our own practices.

Although there are many ways to structure a study group, it is most important to foster a climate in which teachers feel free and safe to participate in the ongoing conversations and exchange of ideas. These study groups should be designed with your teachers in mind. They should focus on the needs of your students and fit the culture of your school. Whether you meet once a week or less often; whether you focus your meetings on a professional book, student work samples, video clips, or a critical question—make the leap into conversation. Here are a few tips to consider as you plan for implementing a study group.

Consider Group Size   Small groups are ideal for study groups, but full-faculty study groups are doable if small-group breakout sessions are an integral part of your planning. You may want to kick off discussion with a general question and then break into smaller groups. Often the optimal number is four to six teachers to ensure there is time for all to exchange ideas. The larger group can reassemble at the end of the session to debrief.

Use Study Questions   Starting with a few questions can jump-start your discussions. There are various ways to use questions.

- Put three or four questions in an envelope and randomly pull them out for discussion.
- Create a chart with two or three starter questions and ask the group to generate more, tapping their own interests and needs.

- Create a list of three or four questions and have teachers prioritize the questions based on the needs of their students.

- Decide on three or four questions and divide the group by interest in the various topics. This allows for a more in-depth study.

- Make copies of the suggested questions for everyone and invite discussion without deciding where to start.

Create an Agenda   Make sure you have planned a beginning and ending time and *always* honor those times. Teachers are busy and knowing there will be a time to start and a time to end is important. Send the agenda to participants prior to the meeting to remind them of the topics to be discussed, as well as any reading to be completed.

Stay Focused on the Topic   State the topic and goals of the session at the start. Plan a procedure that is transparent. You might start by saying something like "Let's decide on a signal to use when we feel the discussion is drifting and then have everyone agree to help stay focused."

Create a List of Norms   Simple expectations that are determined by the group often make study groups function with greater ease and increase potential for success. These can be simple and might include ways to invite a tentative member into the conversation, expectations about listening and sharing, start and stop times, and a procedure for refocusing.

Make It Personal   Make the learning personal for each participant. You might begin each session with teachers turning to a colleague and sharing a quote or teaching idea that resonated with them.

Share Leadership   Rotate group facilitation. Identify several "duties" for the facilitator. Examples might include identifying a question to stimulate discussion, suggesting a big idea from a chapter or group of chapters, posing reflective questions (e.g., "Why do you think the authors kept emphasizing that point?"), and summarizing at the end of the session. Remember that in a study group, *everyone* is a learner. This isn't the place for an "expert"!

Include Everyone   Keep groups small enough so that even the quietest member is encouraged to speak. Active listening on everyone's part will help. Remember that periods of silence should be expected when people are thinking.

Encourage Implementation   Decide on an activity or teaching technique that participants will try with students between sessions. Having tried some of the ideas allows teachers to bring insights to the next meeting and ensures that the study group goes beyond talk and into action.

Engage in Reflection   Stop from time to time to reflect on what you are learning and how you might make your group's interactions more productive. Make sure you take time to enjoy one another and celebrate your learning.

Set Dates for the Next Meeting   Always leave knowing when you will meet again, who will facilitate, and what the general focus will be for the upcoming session.

The following questions relate to the content in each chapter. These are suggestions. Many more concepts and ideas are presented in each chapter. Enjoy!

Guiding Questions

Introduction

1. Why is mastery of math facts important? What problems have you observed when students do not know basic math facts?

2. In what ways would a strong understanding of numbers support students as they focus on math facts?

3. What have you observed about anxiety related to memorizing math facts? Are there types of math fact practice activities that increase anxiety or decrease anxiety?

4. What types of activities might motivate students to practice math facts?

5. How might attention to the sequence in which facts are introduced support mastery of the facts?

Chapter One: Understanding Addition and Subtraction

1. Why is it important for students to understand the concepts of addition and subtraction?

2. What problems might occur if students are asked to memorize math facts too soon?

3. What types of models might be used to help students visualize addition and subtraction? Why might using a variety of models be helpful for students?

4. What real-world experiences might create an effective context for addition or subtraction problems?

Chapter Two: Plus One, Plus Two

1. What prior knowledge will help students better understand +1/+2 and –1/–2?

2. What tools or models help students visualize +1, +2 and –1, –2?

3. Why does it make sense to address –1 and –2 shortly after +1 and +2? What misunderstandings could occur? How will you address them?

4. Reflect on the importance of students' understanding of the commutative property. In what ways will it support their success?

Chapter Three: Adding Zero

1. Why might addition and subtraction with zero be confusing for some students?

2. What might you do to clarify the concepts of addition and subtraction with zero?

3. In what ways does the integration of children's literature enhance math facts lessons?

4. What rules will you establish for managing math fact games within your classroom?

Chapter Four: Adding Ten

1. Why is adding ten an important foundational skill?

2. In what ways might tens facts be challenging for students?

3. How will you help students recognize their successes?

4. What visual tools might help students better understand +10 facts?

5. Why are so many of the activities within the book focused on partner discussions? What are the benefits? What might you consider to ensure success with partner tasks?

Chapter Five: Doubles

1. How might you assess fluency for students who struggle with written Fact Checks?

2. In what ways will visual experiences help simplify doubles facts? What tools provide effective visuals of doubles?

3. Why is it important for students to explain their thinking as you explore sets of math facts?

4. How might using the terms *double* and *half* support or confuse students? What might you do to help them understand the terms?

5. What are the benefits of modifying familiar math fact games for different sets of facts?

6. How might you differentiate tasks for different levels of learners?

Chapter Six: Making Ten

1. Why is it important to allow students time to explore tens?

2. How will a deep understanding of tens support students with other facts?

3. What games and practice activities might support automaticity?

4. Why is this a good time to work on fluency of the already explored facts?

5. How can you ensure that your students will get repeated practice with math facts?

Chapter Seven: Using Tens

1. How will students' understanding of tens support them with more difficult facts?

2. Which activities would be good choices for math fact centers? Why?

3. What management considerations are important when setting up math facts centers?

4. How will you provide repeated practice for students who have still not mastered past fact sets?

5. What planning considerations will make a Family Math Fact Night most effective?

6. What is the role of language in developing math fact strategies?

Chapter Eight: Using Doubles

1. How will students' understanding of doubles support them with more difficult facts?

2. Give examples of some addition or subtraction math facts for which students might use different strategies. Explain how each strategy makes sense for the fact. Is one more efficient than the other?

3. Beyond supporting mastery of math facts, what are the advantages of focusing on number strategies?

4. When are students transitioned from activities to build understanding to practice for fluency? What understandings must occur prior to fluency practice? Why?

5. How might home practice of math facts be beneficial for students? Are there any drawbacks? What can you do to promote effective home practice activities?

Conclusion

1. What are the most significant ways in which we should rethink the teaching of math facts?

2. The authors contend that automaticity takes time. How do some programs rush students as they learn math facts? How can we ensure that enough time is allowed for students to master facts?

3. Reflect on the teaching sequence of math facts within the book. In what ways might this sequence benefit students versus the more traditional sequence of +0, +1, +2, +3, +4, and so on?

4. The authors suggest that effective math fact teaching "cultivates reflective students who have a greater understanding of numbers and a flexibility of thinking that allows them to understand connections between mathematical ideas." Do you agree or disagree? Why?

5. What tips would you give to a beginning teacher who is deciding how to approach the teaching of math facts?

Additional Study Group Resource

Viewing short video clips of teachers and students in real classroom situations generates discussion, conveys new instructional approaches, and promotes reflection about teaching and learning. For authentic video clips related to math fact teaching, try the following resource:

Bureau of Education and Research. 2009. *Increasing Your Students' Mastery of Addition and Subtraction Math Facts.* Bellevue, WA: Bureau of Education and Research.

A Guide to the CD-ROM

The companion CD provides you with a multitude of resources that will simplify your planning and reduce your preparation time as you explore math facts with your students. The activities can be used as they appear or can be modified to suit your needs.

Organization of the CD Files

The CD files are organized into four main sections. Each section contains a variety of files to support you as you explore addition and subtraction facts.

Teaching Resources

This section holds activities specific to the fact set explored in each chapter. The files are divided into two sections: Featured Resources and Additional Resources. In Featured Resources, you will find all of the recording sheets, game boards, and activity templates that are mentioned within the chapter. For each fact set, Additional Resources have also been provided. These games and activities were introduced in a different chapter for a different fact set but have been modified for the new fact set to provide some additional activity options for students' continued practice.

Teaching Tools

Teaching Tools contains many generic tools that can be used for all fact sets. You will find number cards, number lines, ten-frames, addition charts, and many other tools to support students as they explore math facts.

Fact Cards

Three types of fact cards are provided within this section for each set of math facts. The large fact cards are intended for teacher use. Templates for addition and subtraction cards are provided for each fact set. Templates are also provided for small, student-sized fact cards, to allow teachers to easily make sets of fact cards for each student by copying the templates on card stock paper. The final set of fact card templates is for triangle fact cards, to provide a tool to offer combined practice of addition and subtraction facts.

Assessment Tools

Several resources are provided to allow you to assess students' mastery of the facts. A Math Fact Automaticity Interview form is included, with directions for conducting student interviews. A Classroom Observation of Automaticity recording sheet, with rubrics for conducting classroom observations of automaticity, is also included. Three types of Fact Checks are included for each fact set: one focuses on the targeted set of addition facts, one focuses on both addition and subtraction within the targeted fact set, and a third provides a mixed review with current and previously explored facts.

A Fact Check progress graph is also included in this section to allow students to graph their own progress. Students shade the bars to show their number of known facts for each try. Although the graph is designed for Fact Checks with twenty facts, remember that it can be modified for use with smaller quantities of facts. Simply change the numbers in the left column prior to printing out the graph or delete some rows on the graph.

Modifications to CD Activities

This CD holds a wealth of tools and activities that are classroom-ready and aligned with today's math standards. You can simply copy them and begin your lesson. We recognize, however, that our students learn math facts at different rates and struggle with different sets of facts. We know that it is unlikely that one task will provide the right practice for all of our students. A task that is easy for some is simply too difficult for many others. Because these CD files are formatted in Microsoft Word, you are able to quickly modify the activities so they are just right for your students.

If students are struggling with a few specific facts, you might delete some of their known facts from a game and quickly add the ones that they need to practice. If students have already mastered a set of addition facts, add complexity to tasks by inserting subtraction facts or more complex addition equations. Delete portions of a task if time is a factor, change the writing prompts if you'd like to learn something different about your students' thinking, or separate a task into two parts if you'd like to do some today and follow up with more tomorrow. If your students love a math fact game that was designed for +10 facts, simply modify it by inserting doubles facts and have them play it again and again! This CD gives you the power to design tasks that are just right for your students.

Modifying the CD files is quick and easy. Delete or insert in the same way that you would for any Word document. When you are ready to save your file, simply rename it and save it to your computer or another CD. The original CD will not allow you to save changes directly to it, to protect all of the original activities on the CD. Have fun, be creative, and design tasks that are perfect for your students' needs!

A Note About the Representation of the Number Four

Placing the CD activities in a Microsoft Word format allows you to simply delete, add, or change any item to meet the needs of your students. In order for you to customize these activities, we selected a standard font that is available on all computers. While primary students represent the number four in this way 4, standard fonts represent four as 4. Most students are familiar with this representation as it appears all around us on signs at the grocery store, computer keyboards, page numbers of books, etc. It may be helpful, however, to discuss with your students the two ways to represent the number four and to use the 4 representation occasionally in class. Keep in mind, if you want to represent four in this way 4, you can simply delete the 4 when it appears and replace it with a handwritten 4.